VISIONS OF ANOTHER WORLD

VISIONS OF ANOTHER WORLD

The Autobiography of a Medium

Stephen O'Brien

Aquarian/Thorsons

An Imprint of HarperCollins*Publishers*

The Aquarian Press
An Imprint of HarperCollins*Publishers*
77–85 Fulham Palace Road,
Hammersmith, London W6 8JB

Published by The Aquarian Press 1989
5 7 9 10 8 6

A catalogue record for this book
is available from the British Library

ISBN 0 85030 836 4

Printed in Great Britain by
HarperCollinsManufacturing Glasgow

For my mother, Beatrice, and all my friends in both worlds; in appreciation of your love and friendship.

Acknowledgements

My thanks to *Psychic News*, London, and all the people, from both sides of Life, who have so willingly contributed accounts for this volume.

Contents

1. The Spirit Calls   9
2. Silent Watchers   25
3. Whispering Voices   37
4. The Angel of Death   54
5. Revelation   64
6. The Mission Begins   74
7. The Coming of White Owl   80
8. Communications from Beyond   89
9. Séances   107
10. Spirit Children   114
11. Animals Survive Too   136
12. Psychic Powers   149
13. Poltergeist   163
14. Pastures New   174
15. Passing Through the Veil   185
16. Behind the Scenes   194
17. Questions and Answers   208
18. 'Oh Great White Spirit . . .'   222
19. Touching Souls   224
20. The Beginning   236

'I have stood on the mountaintops of the Shining Lands and experienced countless Visions of Other Worlds Beyond Death, and I am not afraid to die; for Death is the Great Liberator, the Bright Angel who leads *all* living things into an Eternal Life, which is their natural birthright.'

STEPHEN O'BRIEN

1

The Spirit Calls

BANG! BANG! BANG! BANG! BANG!

I woke up startled and sat bolt upright in the bed.

BANG! BANG! BANG! BANG!

The sound of ghostly hammering at our front door echoed up the stairway. It was deafeningly loud and I was terrified by it. Who could be calling on us at two o'clock in the morning?

My brother John slept peacefully beside me and so did Uncle Billy across the room. Why didn't they wake up? Couldn't they hear this unearthly noise?

BANG! BANG! BANG! BANG!

I shook John frantically, but he didn't flinch. The ghostly hammering continued. But why didn't mother or father answer the door? Perhaps I was dreaming? Gripping the skin on my arm I gave it a hard pinch and immediately registered the pain — I was wide awake. But I couldn't get up; I couldn't move, I was paralysed with fear.

BANG! BANG! BANG! BANG!

In my childish mind I imagined some hideous monster outside our house trying to get in. He was after *me*, I thought. Then I shot underneath the bedclothes, hiding my face from the night. I knew that if I went to the window and looked down I'd see who it was, but I just couldn't do it. I froze in the bed, clutching at my sleeping brother.

The phantom noise was growing louder now, more insistent on gaining my attention. It echoed through the walls and windows; a hollow, eerie sound. Cuddling up to John, I told myself if I ignored it, it would go away — but it didn't. It continued louder than ever.

BANG! BANG! BANG! BANG!

With my heart pounding in my chest, and sweat upon my brow, I began to tremble. Why was this horrifying noise happening?

Then, as quickly as the phantom hammering had started, it suddenly stopped. I gasped in fright, and waited and listened . . . A deafening silence filled the night.

Calmness fell about the house again, and not a sound could be heard. The ghostly visitor had gone. I don't know how long I sat there in that dark night before I breathed a heavy sigh of relief. I couldn't understand what had happened. Why didn't anyone else get up? The unearthly noise was loud enough to wake the dead. I couldn't figure out an answer, so I pulled the sheets up over my head, clung onto my brother and decided to ask my mother for an answer tomorrow. Half-way through the night I eventually settled down and fell into a deep, troubled sleep . . .

I awoke at dawn. Our small terraced house was lit by the early sun. Quickly, I dressed and went to the window, peering down to see if our phantom caller had left any trace of his presence. But there was nothing. No mysterious footprints or scratchings on the door — nothing but the flowers and the violet dawn-lights.

At breakfast everyone said they hadn't heard the hammering in the night. They said I'd imagined it.

'But I didn't,' I protested. 'It was loud and frightening.'

'Oh don't be silly,' said my mother. 'Who'd be knocking our door at two in the morning? You must have been dreaming, Stephen.'

'But I wasn't! I pinched myself to prove it. Look!' And I showed my mother the pinch-mark on my arm.

'Well,' she sighed, peering at the bruise, 'perhaps someone

got the wrong address. It may have been a tramp.'

'Don't you believe me?' I cried. 'The noise shook the air.' But there was no reply and no more was said about our mystery caller. But that didn't satisfy me — I wanted an answer and was determined to get one. So, that evening, I pulled on my winter coat and went to see old Mrs King. She was a Spiritualist who lived just down the terrace and I was fond of her homely manner and kind ways. If anyone could give me an answer, she could, I reasoned — she knew all about these odd things.

Visiting her was like walking back into Victorian times. Her shabby kitchen was lit only by a few candles and a flickering oil lamp. Everything was gloomy, dark and unkempt on account of her age and infirmities. I entered the musty kitchen and found Mrs King in her usual fireside chair. Lit by the fire's glow she sat all huddled up like a tiny wax doll with withered features and pointed nose, for all the world like a character from a Dickens novel. She would never let me call her anything else but 'Gran'.

'Gran,' I said, 'who was that at our door?'

'Well,' she croaked, 'it sounds like *their* work to me.' And she glared at me over her blue-tinted spectacles. 'It'll be *them* — that's who it is.' Then she mopped up her soup with some bread.

Before I could frame my next question, there was a loud *thud* from the kitchen door. We turned to see what was happening and as we watched, the latch lifted up of its own accord and the battered kitchen door creaked open wide. Yet there was nothing outside but the chill night air. Gran and I exchanged furtive glances.

'Oh, here they are again,' she muttered. 'Go and shut it, Stephen.' As I re-locked the door I remember thinking to myself, 'I don't know why I'm bothering, it'll only open again as soon as I sit down.' And sure enough, it did. With a strangled creak, it unlatched and swung open once more. Gran glowered at me as though it were my fault.

'Well I'll be jiggered!' she said. 'This always happens when you're here. You attract them, Stephen.' So, after closing the door again, it came as no surprise to see it once more defy all known physical laws and open on its own. As I closed it, suddenly Gran's temper exploded.

'Now listen here, you lot!' she shouted at the spirit-people. 'It's got to stop, all this opening of doors! It's alright for you, you can't feel the cold like us! Now give it a rest, will you!'

We waited with baited breath for about a minute, both glaring at the door. Thankfully, it remained shut, so Gran carried on with her soup and continued. 'You see, some folks attract spirit-people like moths to a candle,' she said, 'and you're one of them, Stephen.'

I listened to the old lady seated in the shadows, giving her wisdom so freely and with such sincerity that I was captivated. There she sat, spinning tales about a world beyond time and space; a world to which everyone would go one day, no matter what they believed or what they'd done — everyone lived on into eternity according to Gran. To a 10-year-old boy she seemed like the Oracle at Delphi, a fount of never-ending wisdom. Enthralled by her stories which seemed to belong to a world of long ago, I learned about her visits to the little Spiritualist church at the bottom of Oxford Street where she'd sit in the 'open circle'. She spoke of times she felt privileged enough to catch a glimpse of a spirit-person or hear a sentence from the so-called 'dead' to be given to someone seated around the fire in the church. Gran would then happily pass on her 'messages' as she called them. 'I get bits and pieces,' she'd say, 'but if what I get from the spirit-world helps people, then that'll do me.'

Then she'd furrow her brow and deepen her voice, announcing to any invisible guests: 'But I only want the truth, mind you. I don't want any mischief-makers, nor any fibbers. The truth is all I'll accept, and if you can't give me that then you can go and take a running jump!' And I couldn't resist a smile.

'Now,' she said, 'about that knocking on your door.' I leaned forward in my seat, eager for an answer. She paused and whispered low. 'One thing's for certain, no earthly hands did it.' My eyes widened. What was she saying? She gathered her thoughts together, then looking right at me, almost through me, she said, 'One day, young Stephen — now mark my words. well — one day, you could be a wonderful medium.' There was a pause. What could I say to that? I returned her an innocent look. She took another breath and seemed to be staring over my shoulder.

'There's a North American Indian behind you, telling me this.' I turned quickly but saw no one; yet *someone* was there, I could feel their electric presence so strongly.

'Yes,' said Gran in her matter-of-fact way, 'you're a medium. They'll be waiting for you.' And quite unperturbed she finished off schlurping her soup.

It was getting late, and I hadn't told anyone where I was going, so I fastened my coat and left her in the shadows and dashed out into the night. As I made my way home a million thoughts whirled through my mind. Me? A medium? No, she'd made a mistake. I was only 10 years old, how could *I* be a medium? But then I felt uneasy. I recalled the strange events of the last few days; the phantom hands, Gran's kitchen door unlatching itself — there seemed to be a link there somewhere. Pulling my collar against the sharp wind, my young mind perceived a kind of pattern slowly making itself known. But I dismissed the idea and made up my mind to tell no one at home. I was going to keep this to myself. After all, it's not the sort of thing you could suddenly blurt out.

Entering our home, very glad to get in from the biting cold, I climbed the stairs to bed and had that usual feeling of someone walking behind me. The hairs on the back of my neck had stood on end since I left Gran's and they were still up now. There was no doubt in my mind. Someone had followed me home.

I could almost feel those invisible eyes watching as I quickly undressed and dived under the sheets. Who was out there? Who was it that clamoured for my attention? I didn't look into the room, but my sensitivity told me there were people, watching, waiting . . . but for what? I dared myself to peer out and see them, but I just couldn't do it. I kept my head firmly covered because my young mind was reliving the episodes of those ghostly hands hammering in the night, and the prediction that I'd be a medium one day. It was all too much for me to grasp so, after a while, I tried to relax and get some sleep. Then, just as I became dozy, I felt myself falling down and down. Something was happening to me; I was plummeting down into the blackness of nowhere at incredible speed, whirling and twisting, like a parachute-jump into deep space. I spiralled round and round, falling, swirling, dropping at an immense pace and thoroughly enjoying the whole experience. The lightness and carelessness were marvellous.

Then it ceased abruptly and I immediately realized I was floating up away from the bed. Yet how was this possible? I'd left my physical form sound asleep beneath me, and in my spirit-body I sailed upwards and inspected the ceiling-rose, getting so close that my spirit eyes crossed. I decided to take a look at the water jug on the dresser and before I knew it, I was there, carried by my power of thought. Stopping beside the jug, I at once became aware of two people standing close by. Then, suddenly swamped by an overwhelming childish fear, I was instantly back in my physical body again.

Out in the dark room I knew there was a Red Indian and his squaw near the foot of the bed. I felt their loving, caring presence, arms outstretched towards me. Then everything became heavy and dull and my consciousness was slipping away as I fell into a deep and dreamless sleep . . .

In the days ahead no one mentioned our mystery caller. Everyone seemed to forget him. But I began to wonder why I was the only person woken up by the visitation. And who were those people in my bedroom? Could it be as Gran had said — they're waiting for me? In hindsight I now see there were other unusual things happening to me at times during my childhood. As a young lad I'd sometimes feel strangely dissociated from my family. I'd wonder who I really was and what I was doing here. It was an odd sensation of 'being in the world but not of it'. Once I even asked my mother if I was adopted. 'Don't be silly,' she had said, and life moved on as normal. But little did I realize then that this feeling of 'not belonging on earth' was to haunt me many more times in the years ahead.

I now clearly see I was the only one to hear the phantom hammering because it carried a message for *my* ears only. Even at the tender age of 10, the spirit people were breaking through to reach me. The spirit-world had already brought a powerful message: *Behold, we stand at the door and knock.*

The spirit callers knew then and probably at my birth that they could communicate with me. They could see the years of co-operation and service ahead of us and how every piece of life's jigsaw would fit into its rightful place at the right time. I see now that I was meant to meet certain people to help unfold my mediumship, special people who had set me on a pathway towards greater understanding of life and self and communication between two worlds. For many years, elder discarnate minds had been quietly at work behind the scenes, carefully studying and planning certain events.

With their extended vision my spirit-people could forsee that together we could join two worlds as one and through mediumship dry the eyes of those who would grieve and give hope to desperate souls seeking some light for their pathway. They could forsee thousands of people assembling in theatres, halls and centres to witness our work. They knew then that the vital message 'Man survives death complete with his character and individuality' would be carried to millions over television, radio and the press.

Yet if someone had told me all this in those early years I'd have laughed. I couldn't possibly have accepted it would ever happen to me . . . yet truth is sometimes stranger than fiction.

For someone seemingly destined to become well known, my beginnings were very humble. I was born on a typical British winter's night. The rain lashed down upon our tiny terraced house in Rock Street in the heart of Swansea town, South Wales. And inside our humble dwelling, a few women were fussing around my mother, Beatrice Maude, who was lying on a sofa in the small parlour. She was close to the delivery of her second child. She was secretly longing for a girl; she already had a five-year-old son called John. The contractions of labour were more frequent now so it was decided my father should take John to the cinema while the women did what they had to do. He agreed and they both went off into the downpour.

As torrential rain kept lashing at the parlour window and lightning lit up the sky, loud dramatic thunderclaps drowned out my first cries as I entered the world a few weeks early on Friday 28 January at just after 9 p.m.

Thankful I was all in one piece, but disappointed because I wasn't the daughter she wanted, Beatrice Maude held me close and kissed her second son. I had a mass of thick black hair, was extremely slim, and 22½ inches long. The women thought I looked like a little rabbit.

Shortly after my birth, Dad and John returned and my brother, excited by my arrival, proudly proclaimed: 'I'm going up to the shop to get him a bottle!' But the shops were closed and it was already past his bedtime — so it was pyjamas for him! I'm told my mother and father didn't know what to call me. One wanted Stephen, the other, Neil. So they named me Stephen Neil O'Brien.

By all accounts I was a very lovable child, but also forward and quite determined. At just nine months I astounded everyone by standing up on my own for the very first time, toddling across the room on wobbly legs, collecting my train set and tottering back to my place, plonking myself down with a triumphant smile. All were stunned by my initiative. 'He's been here before,' they said.

I even outsmarted my parents sometimes. At night I'd lower my cot-gate and rip the wallpaper, watching it tear from the bottom right to the top of the ceiling as I pulled it. Very annoyed with me, they moved my cot well away from the walls and my mother tied dozens of knots on the cot-gate with old stockings. That was me safe for the night, or so they thought. When she came up later, there I was — all the knots untied, the cot-gate down and me grinning in the bed waving freshly-ripped wallpaper!

I was a thin toddler and very quick on my feet. When bedtime was announced and my mother frantically tried to grab us both for a wash, she always caught John, but never me. I'd nip out quickly between her legs and out into freedom! But I'd eventually give in and come inside. Every night was our ritual wash-and-pyjama session; my mother would take off our trousers and tops which she'd so painstakingly made from oddments of material and grumble: 'I don't know, you boys can't keep anything in one piece for five minutes.' She'd have found a tear-hole somewhere. We'd be packed off to bed and she'd then hope for some peace and quiet, but she was nearly always disappointed. Hearing the noise she'd shout up the stairs: 'What's all that din?! You'll bring the ceiling through, you two! Stop fighting!' But that didn't deter John and me — we'd carry on bashing with our pillows, knocking each other off the bed amid laughter and flying feathers.

We were two healthy boys, yet we differed vastly in temperament and taste. John liked sport and I was a creative child. However, we loved each other dearly and we worshipped our mother. She was the centre of our lives. If we hurt ourselves, she'd be the one we'd run to for help. She was everything to us; a kind, loving woman — someone very special. In some ways I guess my mother spoiled us. She gave in to our childish whims most times, and though she tried her best to discipline us we only remember her with love. She was a compassionate woman and her great love of people often sent her off to somebody's house or other, helping wherever she could. She used to set ladies' hair, wallpaper old people's houses, and do odd jobs for elderly folk in the town. Once she was almost physically sick; she'd scraped wallpaper off some old lady's walls to redecorate, and there were bugs all over them. Pulling a grimace she said: 'I pasted them back to the wall.' And then she smiled.

My father was completely different. I can't remember the time he ever picked us up as children. He was a distant figure, undemonstrative, and we never really got along well. However, he was a good provider, working as a steelworks' foreman to feed us, but I feared my father's quick and explosive temper. He had very little patience with me, and was more closely associated with my brother.

However, many fond memories do flood back when I think of my childhood, like the time I bought six tins of children's bubbles, and the whole street assembled on a glorious summer's night watching the air filled with these rainbow orbs. We children nicknamed our road 'Bubble Street'.

Rock Street was the kind of place where doors stayed open until way past midnight, and women could be found gossiping on their doorsteps about their daily happenings. The only time the doors closed was when families went to bed and even then they sometimes didn't lock them. It was a close-knit community. Any street fights or squabbles were public property, and people having a fist-fight could expect the whole street to come and watch. When Peter and Jimmy decided to argue over a woman they gathered quite a crowd. The demented woman got between them to try and stop the fight, flailing her arms and screaming, and there was blood everywhere. And the more she interfered, the harder they lashed out until someone in the crowd shouted, 'Leave them alone — they might knock some sense into each other!' That was Rock Street.

Yet in their own simple way the people of our street loved one another. There was an inner respect for family life, a mutual disgust for immoral activities they heard about. And there was always plenty of laughter. I remember when Florrie, our neighbour, put a huge tureen of clear soup on the window sill to cool and just as she lowered it a football landed smack in the middle of it, splattering her and all the windows around! And that's another thing — people spoke their minds; they said exactly what they meant and didn't dress it up either!

Every summer some women would hire a coach, and knock on the doors collecting their money for a day out at Caswell Bay beach. Those picnics by the sparkling sea were marvellous. The coaches were packed, the singing was loud and raucous, and the sandwiches were always full of sand! Trust me to spoil it all by falling from the top of Caswell hill and rolling down to the bottom. I stood up and someone snapped my picture, looking very dazed but happy all the same. John wasn't going to be out-done though, so he swam off into an oil-slick and the women had to butter him all over to remove the thick oil. They were happy times. But then came a shock.

When I was five they packed me off to be educated. I didn't want to go, but they made me do it. Waun Wen School was less than a stone's throw from our house, but it might as well have been a million miles outside the universe, for that's how it felt at first. It was a good school though, with caring staff — all except a ginger-headed, freckle-faced teacher, whose name thankfully escapes me. She'd glower down at us in the infants class, clasping her wooden ruler. Then she'd thrash us wildly across the legs if we displeased her. Some people should never take up the teaching profession.

I wasn't a difficult child, but I was determined, they say; actions spoke louder than words to me, which got me into several scrapes. I remember one particularly. At school we ate our lunch in a damp church hall nearby. The food was delivered by van and we were on the end of the tour. As a result our meals were often luke-warm and very unappetizing. We'd trudge down the line clutching our plates, dropping with hunger and moaning to the well-fed dinner ladies: '*That* doesn't look very hot.' Slopping out potatoes onto the plates they'd rattle back: 'Nothing to do with us, love. We only dish it up.'

Sitting at our tables, toying with our food, we'd often complain to the supervisor. She was tall, thin and mean and had a lightning-quick clip which she could deliver at 10 paces — and often did. 'Miss,' we'd say, 'our food's . . .'

'Quiet!' she'd snap back. 'Eat it up, some children are starving.'

'Yes,' we thought, 'we know what it feels like.'

Well, three of us soon became tired of this. Johnny, Paul and I gathered in the playground and I hatched an inspired plan. We made large cardboard placards and wore them. On them we wrote 'We want hot dinners' and 'Give us warm food'. Then the three of us stomped around the yard shouting our chant for a better deal. We thought it was a smashing idea.

We wanted hot food, but what we actually got was our arms grabbed as we were dragged off to outside the headmaster's study. We stood there, the three of us; a pathetic sight, all pale with hang-dog expressions, clasping our hands behind our backs and eyes lowered.

'Don't feel sorry,' I chirped to the other two, 'we've got a good case.' Suddenly the study door opened and Paul was called in. Johnny and I looked anxiously at each other, not knowing what to expect. There was a lot of muffled talking behind the closed door and then we heard a resounding THWACK! The door opened and a red-faced Paul emerged, clutching his behind, and he ran out into the yard. Johnny and I exchanged fearful looks. Johnny went in. Two minutes later Johnny came out, like Paul, with all the dignity smacked out of him. Then it was my turn.

I stood before our tin god, the headmaster. He eyed me up and down, then raised an educated brow and said: 'So, you're the brains behind this escapade?' Feeling weak at the knees, but not showing it, I bravely answered 'Yes.' There was an endless pause while he cleaned his spectacles, that infuriating habit he adopted when he wanted you to suffer. Finally, he broke the tension and grunted: 'You should have got a petition together, brought it to me and I'd have dealt with it properly, instead of all this nonsense.'

Suddenly I don't know what came over me, and I blurted

back: 'Our dinners are cold. Would *you* like to eat cold food?' I guess that took him by surprise. Adults very rarely treat children with respect but the moment the child shows defiance the adult is shocked. By now I felt I'd stood there 30 years.

'Because you masterminded this plan . . . you can go,' he said. Well, I couldn't understand it, but I didn't wait about for him to change his mind. Just as I was closing the door behind me, I caught him saying, 'You show qualities of leadership.' But I had gone.

We got our hot lunches.

I didn't always get my own way. Every two months John and I were given a shilling after school and ordered to get our hair cut. Down we'd go to a small house owned by ancient Willy Woolard. We'd joke, 'We're off to Woolard's to get our wool cut!' Willy was an amateur barber and his services came very cheap. Looking back, it's easy to see why. There we'd sit with other unfortunate boys all dreading the prospect of facing his scissors. How we loathed this experience.

The door would fling open and Willy would lurch in, dragging his withered leg behind him. His constantly-lit cigarette always had more ash than tobacco on it, and you couldn't escape the smoke if you tried. In one hand he clasped a pair of shears and in the other — the dreaded china basin. He focused his one beady eye upon his nervous victim, then quick as a flash he'd flop the basin on your head and with no skill whatsoever shave right around it. And that was your haircut! Well, you can imagine how I felt. I used to protest until I got a shaped style. After a few initial battles he eventually got the message and asked apologetically: 'How do you want it today?'

'Decent, please,' I'd reply.

If ever I complained my mother would agree to keep the peace and smooth things over, but Dad wouldn't have any nonsense.

'Stop spoiling him will you, Beattie! He'll grow up soft,' Dad used to say.

'Oh leave him alone,' my mother countered, 'he'll make something of himself one day, Ron. Stop picking on him all the time.'

'That boy will grow up dull,' snarled my father, who believed he was always right. 'Let him go and play football like the others.'

'He doesn't like football,' said Mam, 'he's a creative child. For goodness sake stop pestering him all the time. I'm telling you — one day he'll make something of himself. Now leave him alone.' Then my father would mutter something under his breath and go out.

To say Dad and I didn't see eye-to-eye would be a gross understatement. If left together for two minutes we'd fight tooth and nail, and I've lost count of the times my mother stepped between us to stop the squabbling. I was much closer to her and adopted most of her ways. Someone once said we grow in the image of those we love and this was certainly true in my case. My mother taught me the value of being valued, the need to have compassion and to take others' feelings into account. She was approachable and kind, and I loved her with all my heart for this. She loved me too, for I remember one gloriously hot sunny day we all went to school in short-sleeved shirts, but by the end of the afternoon it was bucketing-down with torrential rain; the raindrops were as big as grapes and the ground was steaming where they smashed onto it. All the other children just stood and gawped at the heavens opening. They looked from the sky to their short summer clothes and then with disgruntled faces they ran out screaming into the downpour with no overcoats to keep them dry. And there at the school gate stood my mother, soaking wet and completely drenched; she was waiting with an overcoat to walk me home. I shall never forget her kindness. It is moments like these that bring my mother's love for me warmly to mind.

'Can't have you soaked through,' she said, cuddling me up as we ran home through the downpour, giggling and laughing together. And when we got home she dried me out and made me a bowl of hot soup to warm me up: my Mam was the best mother in the world.

I slowly began to settle into my new routines at school. I had made new friends I never thought existed before! But one morning, something happened to me in the yard that not even my new friends could do anything about. I fell down in pain, clutching my side.

'What's wrong?' they asked. I told them it was nothing, trying to be brave as little boys do. Although I was just eight, I was determined not to be laughed at. But the pain I suffered got worse as the day wore on.

'Stephen!' called out a teacher. 'Stop pulling that ridiculous face and get on with your sums!'

'Yes, Miss,' and I soldiered on without complaint.

After school, all the other lads dashed out of the gates as though their trousers were on fire, as usual. But I just crept along the big school walls. I was in dire agony. What was happening to me? Why did this piercing stabbing keep pounding in my side? I barely had the strength to support myself as I staggered home through the streets. The pain cut deeper — like a twisting red-hot knife inside me.

I leaned on our passage-way walls. I couldn't go any further. As I called out for my mother, the floor came up to meet me in a frightening blur — and I collapsed to the ground. After that, I don't remember much, just snippets of frantic conversation floating over my head. Then blackness, and then more panicky adult talk.

The next thing I knew, my mother grabbed her handbag and some clean pyjamas and we were in an ambulance, shooting through red lights at breakneck speed. In the distance I could hear my mother's urgent voice saying over and over, 'He will be alright, won't he? Please say he'll be alright.'

But that is all I can recall. I was in too much agony to hear the rest; I was slipping in and out of consciousness. I thought I was going to die and recited the Lord's Prayer over in my mind as they rushed me through the huge swing doors of the hospital and an immediate examination was given. 'God bless you, son,' I dimly heard my mother say, as a massive surgeon leaned over me and gave me a painful injection. 'Count to 10, lad,' he said. But before I reached three, I was swamped by the blackness and had gone . . .

I hated the hospital. They put me in a children's ward where the noise was unbearable — I just had to do my best to tolerate it. The doctors said I'd had acute appendicitis and that if they hadn't operated immediately, the appendix would have burst. But that didn't quell my anger about the noise, and as much as the nurses tried to pacify me, all I wanted was my mother. I would look anxiously across at the windows in the ward doors. Who was that behind the frosted glass? Was that *her*?

'Why can't they let her in anytime, instead of these silly visiting hours?' I whimpered pathetically to the staff.

After what seemed like a century's wait, the bell rang out and my mother came in wreathed in smiles. We hugged each other. I was so pleased she'd come. But what was that under her arm? A present! It was a Toy-Town Post-Office Set! All this and love, too! I felt like a king, despite the ache in my side.

I soon felt safe again, but I quarrelled with the nurse when she told me my mother had to leave. I was really upset. 'Sleep, well, Stephen,' said Mam as she kissed me. 'I'll be back again tomorrow to see you.' And then I was at peace. 'Good night, God bless,' she whispered softly. But before we parted, I called her back and gave her a token of my love. I presented her with a Toy-Town letter.

'It's a special delivery,' I said, smiling.

And as she read it, her face lit up and her clear eyes misted over with the love of a mother for her son. For on it, I'd written:

To Mises O'Brien. I love you.

2

Silent Watchers

When I was 10, we moved house. We had to — the road was being demolished under a slum-clearance scheme. So we ended up in Gors Avenue about a mile away; but we couldn't persuade our beloved cat, Tibby, to join us. After all, why should she? She'd ruled the place from the moment we took her in as a tiny scrap, wobbling on weak legs. No, Tibby wasn't having any of this silly moving nonsense! Besides, she had countless gentleman-friends in the district, as her frequent litters proved! In the end she had to be manhandled in two overcoats, shrieking and flaying her claws as we carried her off to our new home. And she soon settled in like the rest of us — blessing the place with yet another fluffy litter!

After all the hustle and bustle of the move had passed, I sat on a tea-chest and prompted by the insecurity of the wrench away from familiar surroundings to somewhere new, asked my mother: 'Mam, what happens when people die? What'll happen to us when we all go?'

After a moment's uncertainty she answered: 'Don't think about such things, Stephen; you're far too young to worry over subjects like that.'

'But I'd like to know about it,' I persisted. So, she pondered . . . 'Well, I believe we'll go on living; *somewhere*,' she said. But I could tell she wasn't sure . . .

Number 22 was a nice place, as terraced houses go, but it was much smaller than our Rock Street home; and (with apologies to Tibby) you couldn't swing a cat in the living-room. It was a two-up two-down affair, which meant John and I shared a room with Uncle Billy, who lived with us, and Mam and Dad had the other room. Trying to sleep at night was an absolute impossibility — positively *everyone* snored, rattled and wheezed! Yet, on the night those eerie hands hammered our door in the early hours, the air was uncannily still, everyone was strangely silent.

After that spirit visitation I guess I became more and more aware of old Gran King's words: 'You attract spirit people like moths to a candle, Stephen'. And glancing back at my childhood I can see my unseen friends were often with me, and sometimes may have even protected me from harm — like the time I climbed over the school wall after hours for a dare with some other boys. Everyone else made the wall, but when my turn came as I reached up to grasp a hand-hold, a huge boulder loosed itself. I saw it come crashing towards me but there was nothing I could do — I was suspended off the ground and couldn't run. I closed my eyes and hunched my shoulders, waiting for impact. The stone came hurtling down on my head, but simply bounced off as if the blow had been cushioned. This could have been the work of spirit guardians, eager I should come to no serious harm, and — even though I carry the dent on my head to this day — no damage was done by this blow which might have sent many young boys into concussion.

I think the spirit-people were also close to me when I was thrown from a 12-foot wall and landed directly on my skull. Old Mr Williams nearby came rushing over, panting for breath and as white as a sheet with shock. He expected me to be unconscious with a broken neck, but I simply got up, dusted myself down and sauntered away totally undamaged. 'I'm alright,' I said.

'Well, I'll go to Hell!' said Mr Williams. 'There's not a mark on him!' And he stood there completely amazed.

Some people believe a blow on the head can instigate psychic vision. I don't know whether this is correct, but on occasions I did see the spirit-people as a child. One morning, glancing through the window, I saw a small girl sitting on our garden wall. She wore a party frock and as I idly admired it she suddenly stood up and jumped from the wall. I shot out of my chair, fearful that such a small child would injure herself with the six-foot drop. But before she reached the ground, she vanished. I was quite taken aback because she had looked so very real to me.

Other times, on hot summer afternoons, I'd sit wearily at the bedroom window, twisting my hair and watching the people walking casually past our house, strolling along. But when they'd get to the brow of the hill, they would often disappear, completely fading away from sight.

None of these visions struck me as odd, so I never felt the need to discuss them with others. I guess children take things at their face value and accept more readily without question. There was never any need for alarm anyway; my spirit-people were always smiling and quite friendly folk.

I think the most startling vision I experienced was what I now know to be called a 'phantasm of the living'. I was visiting Mrs King and gaining more knowledge about these peculiar events. It was a steamy-hot July day, the kind of weather that makes the pavements shimmer with rising heat. We were chatting away in the kitchen, awaiting the arrival of her grandson. I happened to glance across the room, and I saw him passing the big window outside. He was as large as life and bouncing along, making for the side of the house.

'Here he is,' I cried, and I opened the door for him. Mrs King looked at me bewildered.

'But there's no one there,' she gently replied, appearing a little worried about my strengthening powers.

We waited for him a while longer, then I couldn't resist it any more — I went outside into the sunshine to sort him out! But Gran was right, her grandson was nowhere to be seen.

'But I definitely saw him,' I said, and gave an accurate description of what he was wearing. Her face changed, for she had realized what was happening.

'Oh, I expect he's been thinking of coming home,' she replied, hidden wisdom prompting her words. Over a half an hour later, her grandson arrived, chirpily whistling in the bright air. But he was not wearing the clothes I 'd seen him in when his phantasm passed the window.

'Your gifts are getting stronger,' Gran warned. I have had experiences like these several times since, and I've come to believe that our thoughts are living things and, if powerfully projected — even on an unconscious level — they can be seen by sensitive people.

Time moved onward in a hazy, slow way, taking with it happy days and many memories I shall treasure for an eternity. The days of youth were so carefree and full of joyful enthusiasm that even the bad times seem better now through the mist of recollection.

One of the happiest moments my mother and I shared was when I slipped home from school early and fell into her embrace. I had passed my 'eleven-plus' examinations, which meant I had qualified for a Grammar School education. 'I'm so very proud of you, son,' smiled my mother warmly, and the family nicknamed me 'Brains'.

I was to go to the best place in the area according to Dad: Bishop Gore Grammar School for boys. We received official notification and my mother took borrowed money and came home loaded with the clothes they said I should have. She'd spent her last penny on them.

'We must have you looking fine,' she smiled. 'It's not every day someone gets an opportunity like this. Bishop Gore's a school — cap-and-tie place.'

I tried everything on, but she confessed there was only one item she couldn't afford to buy — the school status symbol, a splendid all wool maroon blazer with special crest on the pocket.

'Don't worry,' she said, 'no one else'll have one on the first day, Stephen. They're very expensive. I'll get you one when I can.' And with that she produced a shiny brown raincoat she'd gone into debt to buy. The sleeves had to be tucked well up and the hem shortened. I was 11 years old but so terribly small and thin. I was four feet $10\frac{1}{4}$ inches, according to my school reports. Everything had to be altered to fit me, and my mother did all this work until late into the night.

Finally, the big day arrived. I went on the bus and approached the huge, awesome red-brick buildings. They looked terrifyingly big to such a small lad. After a few awkward moments, I self-consciously entered the gates. A bell rang out and we were shepherded into a quadrangle and made to stand in line, in order of initial. There were 150 new boys that day. I looked around me at them all, and I had never felt more humiliated in my life — 149 boys wore their maroon blazers, and I stood there in my outsize, hemmed-up brown raincoat. I just felt I wanted to die. The experience of going there was bad enough without this added shame.

What is more, I hated the place. It was like a concentration camp. They made us march up and down and into a massive assembly hall where they told us that discipline was the making of a young man. It was awful. I couldn't wait to be released, and when I got home that night I could feel my throat tighten as I reached our house. I belted in through the door, threw my raincoat to the ground, shouted and raved at my mother about the blazer then dashed upstairs, fell onto the bed and sobbed and sobbed and sobbed my heart out. I hated that place.

My mother softly climbed the stairs and sat beside me. 'I'm sorry,' she whispered gently. 'I'll get you a blazer first thing on Monday morning. I'll borrow some more money.'

'I don't want to go back there,' I whimpered. 'I never want to go near that school again.'

She put her hand on my shoulder and squeezed it gently. 'Give yourself a chance, Stephen. Don't be too hasty about this. You'll see. I'm always telling your father you'll make something of yourself one day. I know you can make it.' She told me I'd soon fit in and that I'd learn to like the new life very much. And, despite all my doubts, she was right.

After a few teething troubles, I settled in well and learned to love the place. It grew on me, and I grew on it, and it gradually became a lovely part of my life. Eventually, Bishop Gore Grammar School days held a special place in my heart. I have many happy memories of it, like the way my friend, Mark, and I used to duck out of the compulsory cross-country runs. We'd hide behind some bushes, completely shattered and breathless and then catch the lads up the second time around. Even then we managed to get in last!

I also remember the time our class was queuing up outside the chemistry labs awaiting the master. That fire-hose wheel had always fascinated me. One of the boys started waving it around amid laughter and giggles. I got it off him and pulled the lever — WHOOOOSH! Water gushed out everywhere, soaking the entire queue who scattered and yelped all down the corridor. Mr Leyshon appeared.

'Who made this ridiculous mess?!' he raved. Everyone turned and pointed at me.

'He did!' they chorused, and I got the usual punishment — a gym-shoe across the backside.

We played a marvellous trick on the French Mistress. Henderson, a quiet boy, had his trousers stolen and the poor lad couldn't persuade anyone to tell him where they were. In fact, he was so retiring and shy that the boys lifted him and placed him on top of the cupboard behind the teacher's desk. And there he stayed all through the French lesson. I think she knew he was there but wasn't reacting. Never mind, we giggled at him throughout the class.

Our Science master was really aged and extremely absent-minded. We called him 'Tommy Test-tube'. He would forget things so easily, we wondered how he had managed to live this long. One afternoon, he turned the bunsen burner onto its invisible flame and completely forgot about it. He rambled on in his usual professor-like way and put his sleeve right through the burner. It caught alight amid gales of uncontrollable belly-laughs!

'Boys! Boys!'he screamed. 'Cease this merriment! Cease it at once! It isn't funny!' But *we* thought it was.

I also had a few difficult encounters with the staff. I disliked the Welsh lessons very much. It was such a hard language to learn and to me it seemed 'dead' and 'useless'. I suppose that's why I day-dreamed in this compulsory twice-a-week class. During the mistress's confusion I once raised my hand, a thought having occured to me.

'Miss, have you marked our test papers yet?' I queried. She turned instantly blue. I thought she was going to explode. I was right.

'Get out!' she screamed like a virago. 'Get out! Get out of my class you ignorant little boy! Get out! Get out this minute!' Well I got the message, and sloped off into the corridor wondering what I'd done. Later, she confronted me.

'Well, O'Brien?' she demanded. I just innocently looked up at her. 'Well?' she exclaimed in a rising tone, 'haven't you something to say to me?' After a few thoughts, it struck me she wanted an apology. Another thought hit me too — I had done nothing to warrant such unkindness.

'Come on,' she sneered. 'What have you got to say to me?'

Standing facing her square-on, I replied: 'Nothing. I have nothing to say to you.'

She ordered me off to the headmaster, but when I explained my case he simply shook his head and said, 'Don't do it again.'

I have always rallied against authoritative people, particularly if they try to take advantage of someone younger or more vulnerable. I guess that is why this next memory is so painful to recall.

Mr Walters took us for mathematics and regularly set us impossible problems for homework. One day, in an exceptionally foul mood, he demanded to view our geometry sums. But Lear, one of the class who sat in front of me, admitted he hadn't done them. Mr Walters gave him such a resounding smack across the head that the rest of the class gasped in horror. Lear began to cry.

When it was my turn to be questioned, my face was already red. 'You haven't done it, have you O'Brien?' asked Mr Walters, no doubt gloating over the prospect of another swipe across a victim's head.

'Oh, yes I did, Sir,' I gabbled, frantically flicking through the pages of my jotter-pad. 'It's in here somewhere,' I said, and I became more and more flustered. Mr Walters leaned over me in disbelief, waiting while I pathetically searched for the homework I had not done. I lied to him. And to this day I recall that sense of dreadful guilt and fear I experienced, especially as he gave me the benefit of the doubt and did not punish me. Yet, looking back now, who could condemn a small boy's lie under these circumstances?

I was good at languages mostly and tended to give more time to these than other subjects. But as I got older I was forced into making selective choices about what to study and what to do with my life. I didn't have a clue about what I wanted to be in the future. It was as much as I could do to cope with the present workloads at school and pressures at home from my father, for at this time our relationship was even worse than before. I was an adolescent now and determined to be counted as at least 'living', even if I didn't matter to the dull adult world about me.

Dad and I would hotly disagree on practically anything. If I dared to venture my opinion on topics under discussion he would shout angrily at me: 'What do you know about it? You're only a kid! You don't have an opinion.' That, of course, started another tirade which usually ended with me dashing out of the house with raised voice and doors slamming loudly behind me.

I wouldn't go back to my adolescent years for anything.

Back at school we were marched in to see the Careers Officer. So, reluctantly, we all trudged into his small office one by one, looking like lambs going to the slaughter.

'You're a clown, O'Brien,' he said to me. I don't know exactly what he meant by that to this day.

'Well, lad, what are you going to do with yourself?' he asked.

'I don't know,' I said. When I told him I rather fancied being a pilot or even being involved in space flight, he laughed right at me. I couldn't help thinking, 'Who's the clown now?' He detailed a few opportunities open to me, none of which appealed or made me want to fly out of the room screaming 'Look out world, here I come!' Then he gave me permission to leave. But before I did, he launched a surprising remark.

'Well,' he said, 'there's hope for you yet, O'Brien. Out of the hundred boys I've interviewed, so far you're the only one who has had the courage to look me in the eye right through it.'

John and I were now at that strange age-gap when he was almost a man and had his own life to follow, and I was still a teenager deep in the throes of uncertainty, as most youngsters are at that age.

The pressures were increasing all the time, but I found some relief in joining the school choir which gave excellent concerts and allowed me the chance of pursuing one of the great loves in my life — music. How I craved and yearned for a piano.

'But Stephen,' said my dismayed mother, 'we just can't manage the cost. I can't afford a piano stool at the moment, let alone a piano; I'm still trying to pay off the loan for your school clothes.' So I was left with a song in my heart, and nothing to play it on. Now I can see we were quite poor really, just scraping a living from day to day . . .

At 16, I was about to face sitting my major examinations. I couldn't really be bothered with studying much at that time. I wanted to enjoy life and living, I wanted to run free and feel the great pulse of life in my veins. So it wasn't difficult to accept Mark's offer of coffee at his home one evening, rather than reading up history. But little did I realize that this was to herald my next contact with the spirit-world, one that would leave a deep impression upon my mind for the rest of my life.

I arrived at his plush home in the west of the town, taking off my shoes so that the carpets wouldn't be marked. We chatted cordially until his mother went out.

'Behave yourselves now, you two,' she said a with a smile.

The door closed behind her and suddenly Mark became conspiratorial. He whispered out: 'Check the coast, and get some kitchen chairs.' I obeyed, not knowing what he was going to do. He pulled the curtains, dimming the light in the room. I placed the chairs opposite each other and he produced a ouija board, a board with the letters of the alphabet around it.

'I've just got this,' he said. 'Let's have a go.' So we placed it between our knees just as the instructions said. Then a thought struck me: 'What if your mother comes back and catches us?' I rattled.

'Shh! Just concentrate on it,' rebuked Mark. So we placed our fingers lightly on the pointer and it immediately sped around the polished board. It spelled out something, and we could hardly contain ourselves, it was very exciting.

S–T–E–P–H

'Stephen!' I shrilled out. It shot across to the 'YES' and made fast, thrilling sweeps around the board again.

'Well, what do you want?' I gasped, holding my throat with my free hand. The pointer seemed just as excited as we were. It whizzed past all the letters as if it were getting used to the experience and thoroughly enjoying it.

'Just look at it go!' squealed Mark. 'It's fantastic!'

'We only touched it and it started straight away,' I added between breaths.

Then, all at once, the pointer stopped. There was a brief pause. 'Is it me?' I questioned. 'Is it me you want to speak with?'

Y–E–S

In disbelief we watched the pointer move. We were riveted with tension and anticipation awaiting a message. What was it going to say? Was it good news?

I AM A FRIEND
I BELONG TO STEPHEN

Mark and I looked at each other, lost for words. 'Well ask it something, Stephen,' he cried. 'Don't just sit there looking dumbfounded — open your mouth and talk!' So I spoke the first words that came into my head.

'How many exam passes will I get?' I asked.

SIX, said the spirit-people.

'And what about Mark?' I continued.

SIX, said the board again.

Well neither of us could believe that; we hadn't studied hard enough, so we knew that prediction was absolute nonsense. But before we could question the Other Side further, Mark's mother came home unexpectedly and we dashed about setting the room to rights so that she was none the wiser about our activities.

'We'll never get six passes each, Mark,' I laughed. 'We're much to silly for that!' Or were we? We would have to wait and see . . .

Soon, the telling moments arrived. Mark and I sat among the 150 boys taking the examinations in the huge assembly hall. This was to be the first of nine three-hour papers. The thought of that ouija board seance was furthest from my mind — I was far too concerned with facts and figures to even remember the prediction by my 'friend'. However, several weeks passed by and the results were posted to us. After the summer holidays, Mark and I got together on the first day back at school. I was bursting with curiosity.

'Well, how many passes did you get?' I quickly questioned. Mark pulled a face and rather shamedly admitted: 'Just one — how about you?'

'Three,' I said, and we both exploded with laughter because the Other Side were wrong. The ouija board predicton caused further giggling that day.

But the spirit-people had the last laugh. When Mark and I re-sat the examinations, he obtained a further five and I added three to mine. That meant we both had gained six passes each. SIX — just as my unseen 'friend' had accurately foretold. But how on earth could the Other Side have known? How could *anyone* have known? Yet, there was no doubt about it, they were right. As strange as it seemed, somehow

   they knew my pathway;

   they were watching;

they were waiting.
And I couldn't help remembering those phantom hands hammering on our front door at two in the morning, six years earlier. And over and over in my mind, one phrase kept tumbling around and around:

Behold, We Stand at the Door and Knock

Unseen, we may be.
Unknown, we're not:
     Yet we're watching the path that all souls tread;
     We once walked there on the Earth ourselves:
And now
We're far from dead.

So listen,
Carefully,
And be aware, my friend:
     For we are near;
     Sweeping the face of your life's clock:
Behold, we stand at the door and knock.

3

Whispering Voices

The insides of the dark bedroom windows were ringed with ice, as swirling snows covered gardens and streets outside in the black velvet night. But I was snug and warm in bed when the sun shone through the blueness and woke me up on Christmas morning. And even though I was 16, there at the foot of the bed was my usual stocking full of fruit and nuts and an old pillow-case containing new clothes. Little did I appreciate then that Mam and Dad had spent their last pennies on those gifts. It's only now, in later years, that I realize just how deeply my mother loved us children. She worked very hard indeed, and went without to keep us clean and fed, her compassionate mind always putting us first if there wasn't enough to go around.

I shall always be eternally grateful for the privilege of having such a wonderful person for my mother. And through her powerful motherlove, I'm convinced she also had a special kind of healing power. Near one Christmas-time when I crushed my thumb, she gently held my damaged hand, and when her soft voice said: 'Here, let me kiss it better for you,' she seemed to soothe the throbbing pain. And, afterwards, my new thumb-nail grew quite quickly.

'Mam, I do love you,' I said. 'I really do.'

'I know,' she smiled back warmly, 'and I love you too. And God knows, Stephen, no matter where life takes us in the years ahead, I'll always help you whenever I can; don't forget that.'

'Oh, I won't,' I promised, kissing her cheek.

'I only hope that I'll live long enough to see you two boys settled down. That's my dearest wish.'

I thought that was an odd thing to say, but I shrugged off the remark, for Christmas meant special treats and thinking of distant family relatives.

I was very close to my grandparents — not on my father's side, but my mother's. Dad's father had died before I was old enough to have known him and by all accounts he was a good and honest man, having educated himself and got on in life through book-learning and hard work. I did, however, know my father's mother quite well. She was Mary-Jane Rees, but everyone called her Polly. She was a tubby, short, fussy woman with a squeaky voice and every Christmas Eve I was taken by my father to see her.

Her home was quaint and full of ornaments she'd collected over the years; none of them very valuable, but all of sentimental meaning. The only problem with Polly was that she was rather mean with her money. She had five sons — my father being one of them — and there was such difficulty with two of them in getting work and conforming to normal standards that she would lock the food cabinet with a padlock to prevent them eating: 'If you don't put money *into* the house, you don't take anything *out*!' she would admonish them.

She was rather pitiful really, as I remember her. She had no end of bother trying to keep her boys in order, and because of the endless bickering and fighting, my Dad ran away from home at 14 and joined the Navy. He told me in later life that he just couldn't stand the atmosphere any longer. Poor Polly was distraught. There she was with four sons, no husband, and endless cares and worries drove her further and further into her usual state of, 'Oh, God, I don't know what I'm going to do, really I don't.'

At Christmas-time when I arrived, the greeting was always the same. She would wipe her hands on her pinafore and throw her arms around me, squeezing me and cuddling me up with all her might and then she'd cry and cry as she exclaimed, 'Oh,

you're wonderful. If only your grandfather could see you now!
You're so smart, you're a real swank. Your grandfather would
be so proud of you, boy.' And she'd hoot and howl away for a
good few minutes before we'd settle down for a cup of tea.

After she and Dad had exchanged family chit-chat and
discussed the welfare of one of his brothers, Mervyn — who was
very ill and undergoing constant treatment — we would rise to
leave, as Polly put on her Salvation Army bonnet and cloak to
go off to her beloved 'meeting'. She used to sing the Temple
down and join in the gossip between the hymns.

Many years later, I heard that at her funeral it was mentioned
to the boys that her favourite hymn was something to do with
'hidden in the cleft of a rock'. The next day, two of Dad's
brothers practically took her garden wall apart searching for
any concealed money. I don't know whether that's true or not,
but that's what I'd heard.

My mother's parents were much closer to me and I do recall
them both with great and deep affection. Mary-Ann and Albert
were two of the most sincerely lovely people a soul could ever
wish to meet. They had been childhood sweethearts, meeting at
school in Tredegar — a small Welsh town — and marrying
quite young. They were very good-looking, too, in their
younger days.

Mary-Ann was a hard-working woman who bore Albert eight
children, seven of whom survived. There were always several
sittings at their terraced house for each meal of the day,
especially when all their children brought their own offspring
on flying visits.

Albert, my grandfather, was a gentle, lovable man. He was
just like my mother. In fact they were like two peas in a pod and
when people say I have his nature and his ways I consider this
the highest of compliments. He was a good soul who used to
walk on the mountains and hills, humming little tunes he'd
made up himself. He would plod along, not letting anything
worry him or disturb his inner peace. On long walks down
country lanes and over grassy slopes, he would contemplate all

manner of things. He was a simple man, with simple needs and his great gentleness truly marked him out as a gentleman.

I was over the moon whenever my mother took us on the bus to spend a week at Nana and Grancha's, as they were known. Mind you, the three-hour bus journey was not a pleasant experience, when we travelled over half-finished country roads and always seemed to get Dr Death as a bus-driver. You know the one — the madcap speed-lover who hits every bump in the road.

Nana and Grancha Price lived near to a disused viaduct which towered up to the heavens close to the back of their house. It had nine incredibly huge arches supporting it. The 'Nine Arches' had a stream running underneath them where my cousins and I would go fishing for 'tiddlers', which we put into jam-jars and then returned to the water later. Further downstream there was a weir and we children would swim in the waters, splashing and dancing about on boiling-hot spring days. It was such fun and the memories of those childhood moments fill my mind with happiness. 'Have a good splash!' my mother would shout.

It was after such a swim that we trundled home across the fields to Nana's house, tired and weary, with the relentless sun beating down upon our bare backs. We crossed the stiles and I fell. My foot caught on a stone and I tumbled headlong into a three-foot high patch of stinging-nettles. I was stung from head to foot; I had stings in places where other people didn't even have places. The women covered me with 'blue-bag', an old-fashioned remedy for all complaints. I must say that by the end of the exercise I looked like 'The Thing from Outer Space'. That wouldn't have been so bad if that was all that had happened to me that day, but I'm afraid I had to top that by falling fully-clothed back into the river. Happy days!

Every time we visited Nana and Grancha, we would always take a bus trip to see one of their other son's families — my Uncle Clifford and Auntie Charlotte's children. They had a big family, and I guess I often thought of the children as the brothers and sisters I would have liked at home.

Aunt Charlotte was a small German woman, wiry and full of life, with a most peculiar accent which I loved to hear. Her jet-black hair used to be arranged in the 1940's style of straight down the back and fluffed-up on top of the head.

'They used to say I was an old witch,' she related. 'Back in Germany, in the War, I'd read my sister's cards and tell her if the soldier she'd arranged to meet that night would turn up or not. They didn't believe I could do it, so they checked me out — and every time, the cards were right.'

Fascinated by her tales, I asked if she'd read the cards for me. She readily agreed and spread out the shuffled deck. And she was remarkably accurate! What's more, she showed me how to do it.

'You've got a funny kind of power with you,' she said, and instructed me on her methods. I was only young, and thought I'd master this skill to show my friends in an idle moment. I thought it would be a real treat for them. But little did I realize that this treat would turn out to be very popular and frighteningly accurate. It was to be another contact with my unseen 'friend'.

I soon found I didn't need the cards at all when people were seated in front of me. I'd mysteriously receive strong impressions, phrases and mental pictures to relay to the sitters. It was only done for fun and there was no payment made, yet people began talking about these sessions and word quickly spread.

One lady was told she was expecting a child. 'I most definitely am not!' she protested.

'Check with your doctor,' I heard myself saying politely. And I was right. The following morning her pregnancy test proved positive. What was supposed to be fun suddenly had overtones of seriousness creeping into it. Nevertheless, being just 16 I carried on, unaware of the deeper implications of the exercise. I also gave a Scotswoman such extremely personal details of her family's secrets that I was instantly whisked off to Glasgow to be put on display at her private home. I needed the holiday, and so didn't mind helping a few people on the way.

They paid my fare and I went on the coach from Wales to Scotland. I don't think I have ever experienced such a gruelling trip in all my days. It was 18 hours long and I just shivered and shook all the way there. My insides were like jelly and when I got off the coach, I had to be helped to stand. My first lesson in 'sacrifice in order to serve' had been well and truly driven home.

From her private house, news soon got around about the young Welsh lad who was 'gifted'. They came from miles away but were all warned by the hostess: 'If you don't like the truth, stay out of there, because that's all he gives.' Even boys from the roughest, toughest districts in Glasgow scrubbed themselves clean, donned suits and paid a visit — but they couldn't get in. I was fully booked.

In the end, I would place the cards down as a matter of course, but not consult them at all. I just worked from my feelings and impressions. I'd get strong sensations, presences moving around me, hands touching me and unseen people whispering to me.

What on earth was happening? Was the spirit-world in touch again? I supposed that it was, so as quickly as reading the cards had come into my life, just as quickly I let them slip out — not fully understanding that they'd been another bridge-head consolidated by the Other Side, ready for our partnership in the years ahead.

When I later told Aunt Charlotte about my experiences, she said, 'If you don't feel right about doing these things, Stephen, then best leave them alone until you're older.' Sound advice. The only trouble was, the Other Side weren't listening to it; or if they were, they certainly were not taking any notice. It seems they had another 'happening' planned while I was staying at my Aunt's home. I can see now that with the onset of puberty my psychic powers were increasing, and the people in the Beyond were going to make the most of this new supernormal energy at their disposal.

My cousin, Ilona, and I were sitting up gossiping late one night. Although it sounds like a scene from a thriller movie, the next 'happening' occured as the clock struck midnight. We had been discussing spooky stories, so our minds were already firmly directed towards the people in the spirit-world, and this must have given them the opportunity they needed.

Ilona was seated upon an old-fashioned three-seater sofa. It was extremely heavy and cumbersome and would take a good deal of push to move it. Yet, although she was perched right on the edge of the seat, it suddenly swung right around into the middle of the room, completely on its own. Ilona's face was a picture.

'What does it mean?' she asked. I was speechless. A few seconds before, we'd been chatting calmly and the next moment this weighty sofa came lurching right across the room towards me.

Just then, there was the sound of footsteps clicking up the garden path outside . . . A key turned in the lock, and the front door swung open. We nearly died on the spot . . .

It was my Uncle Clifford! I don't think I could describe our great sense of relief, even if I tried. Uncle Clifford had just finished his night shift at the steel furnaces where he worked. We didn't mention anything to him, but we both explained it all privately to Aunt Charlotte the next day.

'They don't interfere with this world without a reason,' she wisely educated us. Aunt Charlotte was quite correct. This was a warning . . .

Within a short time Uncle Clifford was blown up in an accident at the furnace and put in a private hospital room to die. But amazingly he made a miraculous recovery, much to his consultant's surprise. I can only assume my invisible 'friend' had forseen the event and used it to prove his presence again.

Back at school, I felt that if I read another book or attended another lecture my mind would burst wide open; so I left at 17. But the following day the Head of the English department called at the house to persuade me to return, for he felt I was worthy of a university education. Weakly, I gave in, and dragged myself back the next day; but after that — my mind was firmly made up. I gladly danced home out of the school, but Dad ordered me to get a job. 'If *I've* got to work, *everybody* works,' he bellowed.

'Find yourself a decent position, Stephen,' cautioned my mother. 'I'm sure you'll find something if you walk the town.' So, to keep the peace, and much against my wishes, I agreed.

'That's the spirit,' encouraged my mother. 'Good luck, son.' And so I sallied forth reluctantly, dragging my heels, and trudged the town and got a position in a swish jeweller's shop. 40 hours a week for a pittance — and it was slave labour in my eyes. We were all dressed up serving the rich, and we staff were practically on the poverty-line.

To say I was bored would be the understatement of the century. I was out of my mind with the wearisome tasks; it was not a good time at all. However, there were one or two lighter moments to ease the insipid atmosphere. Maisie, a scatter-brained assistant, took me by the arm and said, 'Observe.' I was supposed to be learning how to deal with the public. She confronted a fur-coated customer, dripping with jewels, and make-up as thick as plaster layered over every available space. She handed Maisie a diamond ring and demanded it be cleaned.

'Certainly, *Madam*,' responded Maisie with a wide smile. I thought her face was going to crack with the over-exaggerated effort.

Downstairs we went, Maisie telling me she would demon-strate how to clean up a valuable ring. We arrived in the tiny kitchen used by the staff — it wasn't plush and carpeted with good-quality pile like the public areas. She popped the ring into a glass of hot water drawn from the tap. 'There,' she said. 'Give it a minute to soak and then I'll show you what to do.' With that, she took some green washing-up liquid, squirted it onto a toothbrush and scrubbed the diamonds willy-nilly. I was agog! It's a good job 'Madam' hadn't seen the proceedings!

One day, there was an electric thunderstorm. A lightning bolt

struck the shop's roof just as I was making my way outside with
a customer to view a watch in the window. I jumped out of my
skin and squealed, and ran back into the store. The management were not pleased. But there was no time for a scolding, the
store basement had flooded, raw sewerage pouring up through
the toilets and covering the cellar floors. The Manager,
'Creepy' Morgan, appeared from nowhere — that's why they
called him 'Creepy' — and sent me downstairs with a bucket.

'Clean it up,' he said. Then he pulled a most astonished look.
I think he must have seen my face when he gave the order.
Anyway, down I went to start this filthy job. There was
sewerage everywhere, and the stench was vile. I collected two
buckets and poured them back down the toilets and suddenly
thought, 'I'm a sales-assistant, not a plumber.' So I trotted up
the stairs and confronted 'Creepy'.

'I don't want to do this,' I announced, and handed a very
surprised man, a dirty bucket.

'Oh, you don't want to do it?' he replied, raising his eyebrows
off the top of his head.

'No, I don't,' I said. So *he* took the bucket, and *I* got the sack.

'Thank Goodness for that,' I sighed as I walked out into
freedom, happy to be out of that establishment, so full of
hypocrisy.

I couldn't understand why everyone was so upset about my
being out of work. They wanted to pressure me into slavery,
but all I wanted was to be free. I'd been cooped up in school for
12 years and now I wanted to be as free as a bird, going
wherever the breeze took me — so that's exactly what I did.

In the evenings I joined an amateur theatre group, getting
quite involved in various shows and having a marvellous time. I
was playing 'Buttons' in a pantomine to a packed hall of 300
screaming children enjoying a matinee performance when, all
at once, I realized the 'Ugly Sisters' hadn't arrived on stage.
They'd missed their cue. What on earth could I do now? There
I was, standing before 300 children, all alone. In the wings I
could hear frantic people scampering about, whispering,

'Where are they? They're supposed to be on!' 'Get them quick!' ordered someone else. To make matters worse there was no prompter in the wings.

Then, quite out of the blue, a small voice inside my head spoke clearly to me. 'Tell them that joke about the super-market,' it said. I instantly recalled the joke and delivered it to the audience, who fell about laughing. They loved it! They roared with laughter and just as they finished, two partially-clothed Ugly Sisters were flung on stage, red-faced and abashed. If it wasn't for that whispering voice the show could have come to a standstill.

In the dressing-rooms afterwards everyone patted my back, congratulating me on my quick thinking, but I didn't tell them what really happened ... they probably wouldn't have believed me anyway.

Soon afterwards, I was elected Chairman of the Youth Theatre, becoming totally responsible for running it. And my first decision was to entertain handicapped people. We got a pianist in, who hit more cracks than notes, and rehearsed old-time Music-Hall numbers for weeks until we were ready. Then we visited a local society.

The handicapped people there ranged from about six years upwards and they were so pleased to welcome us. They gathered round the stage, and watching from the wings we were immensely moved by their courage and fortitude in bearing their grave disabilities. Nurses wheeled people into position; some wore callipers, others were carried to their seats. Some sat themselves down, eager to hear the concert, but unable to speak. Some were blind.

Watching from the tiny wings, I found myself quietly uttering, 'Dear God.' And Linda close by said, 'It must be awful for them, Stephen.' I couldn't find the words to express how I felt. 'Heart-breaking,' was all I could say.

We pulled ourselves together, roused the cast and, with no scenery, plenty of flat notes and bags of youthful enthusiasm, we started the show. It was a lively production, but only half-produced really. Nevertheless, after many successful chorus numbers, duets and solos, we were completely overwhelmed by the cheers and clapping we gained. They'd thoroughly enjoyed themselves. Especially the 'Alexander's Rag-Time Band' number, where we all played imaginary instruments. We had to do that one twice!

A nurse stepped forward amid the cheering and said, 'Thank you for coming. So many people forget about us.' Moved to an encore, more happy singing followed and the audience loved it. They stamped their feet and clapped and sang along, even pulling us out to dance a much-welcomed Conga.

It was a night full of laughter, tears and great satisfaction, having entertained people less fortunate than ourselves. Seeing those happy faces and listening to the cries of delight made me decide to help physically and mentally handicapped people again in the future.

When the show finished, we could barely leave the building. There was a mad dash to thank us. Our hands were shaken, our coats were pulled and there were calls of, 'Please don't go.' Suddenly, a small dark-haired lad who could barely stand was thrust forward by the crush, and he clasped me firmly around my chest, smiling and chuckling, so grateful for our visit. His hug was so tight I could scarcely breathe.

'God bless you,' I said. But there was no reply. I looked into his young eyes. There was a most wonderful light in them, and to this day I'll swear he was a great and noble soul, trapped in a tired, unresponsive body.

'It's been a lovely night,' I said, meeting his smile with mine. 'What's the matter, cat got your tongue?' I asked. A nurse touched my arm.

'He can't speak,' she whispered. 'Hugging you's the only way he can say, "I love you".'

I held him tightly, my lips trembling, tears welling in my eyes. I couldn't speak a word back to her. There was a lump in my throat. If I'd tried to say something it wouldn't have made any sense I'm sure.

Finally, after many hugs and fond handshakes, we said our goodbyes and, deeply moved, we made our way homeward.

My mother was sitting by the fireside reading her newspaper.

'How did it go, Stephen?' she asked.

'Oh, fine,' I said. But my face gave the story away. I was soon telling her all about the soul-stirring evening's events.

'I'm proud of you,' she replied. 'If you can help someone less fortunate than yourself, then that's what life's all about.'

Her loving words echoed through my mind as I lay in bed that night, pondering over the show and its effect on those people. It was then I firmly set my mind on doing something to help people in need. I didn't know exactly *what* I would do, but I just knew I'd do something in the future.

The next day over coffee at Linda's, we discussed the concert.

'Fantastic work,' she cried, 'and everyone was pleased.' I heartily agreed and we joked about the songs that went wrong, and people who'd missed their cues, leaving the stage embarrassingly empty, much to the delight of the audience.

As we chatted, a most odd experience occurred. I suddenly felt as though a blow had struck my head. Not a pain, but an electric shock to the left side of my brain. And in that instant I knew someone had been hurt. I clasped my head and cowered in my seat. Linda looked bewildered. I quickly glanced at the clock and saw it was three o'clock.

'Somebody's been hit,' I called out, 'struck on the head.' Linda returned a hard, piercing glare. 'Have you gone mad?' she asked. But later that day I decided to check out this psychic experience. I questioned my mother first.

'Don't start all that again, Stephen,' she said. But undeterred I did the same with Dad and Uncle Billy, but drew blanks in each case. Then I asked my brother.

'How did you know that?' he barked at me, very much the young man. But my explanation fell onto deaf ears. Nevertheless, at three o'clock that afternoon he'd been loading heavy crates onto a lorry when an iron girder fell, striking him a glancing blow to the left side of his head.

'Someone told you about it!' he cried, not wanting to believe my true story. But by now I'd learned not to argue. They could dismiss me as much as they like, but I knew what I experienced, and I also knew that no one could take that away from me. I didn't fully grasp the mechanics of the happening then, however; but now I feel that it took place because we do have a psychic link with those whom we love, whether they are in this world or the next. It is a kind of magnetic link that can never be broken, a thread of awareness that somehow ties us to each other. When our loved ones are distressed, a sensitive relative can register this, and distance is no object.

So, had John mentally called out to me? Did he think of me the instant the blow struck? He wouldn't say. But whatever happened, the impressions certainly reached me — the millisecond they occured. Just as they did in this next recollection.

One of the theatre group members was a young girl called Marie. Tired of living at home, she decided to branch out and get herself a flat. When she found one, several of us trouped along to give it a clean and help her out while she went through the process of settling in to her new place. It was an old building, probably built in Victorian times, and she had procured the downstairs apartments. They were not in very good condition, and I spent some time painting the woodwork for her. During our chats together, Marie told me that she thought she was being 'pursued' by 'something inexplicable'. Upon questioning her further, she believed the flat was haunted and that whoever was there was intent on troubling her. She told us tales of her bad psychic experiences there, which we neither fully accepted nor rejected. To be honest, we didn't know what to make of it. I, for one, kept an open mind. At 17, what else could I do? What did I know of hauntings and such like? I was certainly no authority on them. So, we comforted her, instructed her to forget all about it, and that was the end of that — or so we thought. Again, I had failed to realize in my youth that the powers generated by my mediumship were beginning to flower, and in this case burgeon.

Right along my young pathway, as I look back over my shoulder, the pieces of some inexplicable plan seem to have all fallen into their rightful place. I didn't ask for the phenomena I experienced in these former years, they just sort of happened. Yet each psychic link seems to be another piece of the jigsaw of my existence. And everyone knows that jigsaw pieces only fit comfortably into one slot. Shortly to come was another piece of the picture, helped and directed into position by the Other Side. . .

It was 2.20 in the morning. I awoke suddenly. It was pitch black in the bedroom, but what was that noise? Who was crying so pitifully? It sounded like Marie — but she lived five miles away, so how could it be? How could I possibly hear her whimpering and sobbing in my room, when she lived so far away?

The sound seemed to be registering in the middle of my brow. I was thrown into utter confusion. I didn't understand what was taking place. Then, at once, I realized — 2.20 a.m. Now I knew why Marie was crying out, screaming to me, 'I'm frightened! I'm frightened! It's back in the room again!' She was being 'haunted'.

Not quite understanding why we could communicate like this, I transmitted my voice to her. As I spoke the soft words of comfort, they seemed to be echoing down a void, a blackness, some kind of cavern — I can't really explain it.

'Don't worry. Go to sleep,' I said. 'It's all over now.' And with that, her voice faded out. But had the spirit entity gone? I could only hope so. Had Marie heard my voice responding to her in that early morning? Could she have heard me as clearly as I had definitely heard her? I'd find out the next day.

I drifted back to sleep with thoughts of Marie's story in my mind. How, at a quarter past two each night, the doorknob of her bedroom began twisting and rattling. How she was terrified by the appearance of a spirit woman who seemed to want to possess her, body and soul. All I could promise myself was that I'd visit her tomorrow to investigate.

The next day, Marie reported back — word for word — exactly what I had transmitted to her the previous night. The five miles that separated us were no barrier to the psychic emanations we sent out. There was no doubt in our minds whatsoever, we had been in pure telepathic contact. While we discussed the whys and wherefores, suddenly Marie screamed out. She'd felt the spirit woman drawing close to her again. And with that, my back sensed the entity approaching along the outside wall. All at once, the form glided into the room and transfixed our gaze. We froze.

Neither of us knew what to do. There, in the doorway, stood a woman, dressed in long, grey draperies. Her white hair tumbled down to below her knees. She stood six feet tall, and oozed selfishness and emnity. Her eyes took in the room, darting from side to side, weighing up the situation. She paid particular attention to me, and then — quite suddenly — she floated over towards an alcove. And, with a burst of sudden hatred into the psychic atmosphere, she disappeared through the recess. We both saw her clearly, and we both guessed there must have been a doorway just there when the house was originally built.

Slowly we regained our composure, and that took quite a time. As emotional balance returned, I found the strength to just about make myself audible. 'I believe you,' I said.

There was no doubt about it, action had to be taken.

That night, Marie, six friends and I trundled into her flat laden with blankets and thermos flasks in hand. None of us had told our parents what we were doing, but we were going to spend the night in the haunted premises. Looking back now, we must have had some pluck; many adults wouldn't have been so brave. We were intending to sit up, absolutely alert, keeping a special look-out at about 2.15 a.m.

All rather young and afraid of meeting the apparition square-on, we exchanged some spooky conversation before settling down about 1.45. Everything was peaceful and quiet, but we were so uncomfortably hot — none of us had undressed in case we had to make a speedy get-away.

We didn't have long to wait. At 2.15 exactly the room felt icy-cold as I registered the spirit's presence approaching from the hall. Marie gasped: 'She's coming!' The others thought we were playing a game, but we were far too frightened for that: we were deadly serious.

Quickly, the spirit moved into the room. She wasn't visible this time but her presence was incredibly strong. Marie screamed and began flaying her arms about as if pushing someone away.

'She's moving round me!' she yelled emotionally, her voice fraught with fear. 'Go away! Get away from me! Tell her to go away!'

I rushed over to her as fast as I could. No one else moved, they were petrified. The apparition emitted a dreadful feeling of intense hatred as I got near to Marie to protect her. When I enclosed Marie in my two arms, forming a circle of light about her, the spirit woman went wild. She circled round and round us with ever-increasing speed, but she couldn't get near to her victim. To this day I don't know why I made this barrier with my arms, or even why it worked, but it did.

The tighter I gripped Marie, the faster the spirit went. She was furious I'd interfered with her plans. Marie was shaking with fear, perspiring profusely, tears streaming down her face. 'Get her away from me! Get her away!' she kept crying out continuously. The others were stunned into silence, totally unaware of what we could sense, yet terribly afraid just the same. Angered and frustrated, the spirit rushed out through the alcove again — so we took our quick get-away. We ran like the wind out into the street and eight of us piled into a freezing-cold car, where we spent the remainder of the night — wide awake.

As we gradually returned to normality, Marie and I cast a quick glance at each other simultaneously. We had both received an identical picture in our minds at the same time. The Other Side had obviously interfered with the proceedings, and we were both shown the spirit woman removed from the premises. And in that instant, we knew all was safe.

Looking back now with maturity on my side, I can see that Marie's highly-strung nature, plus her own innate psychic abilities, allowed this mischievous entity the pleasure of provoking a young girl into hysterical behaviour. The spirit visitor produced terror and tears for sheer amusement and morbid pleasure. The episode highlights, however, that mediums and others involved in the psychic fields don't always find love and light in the Beyond. Everyone survives death, and there must be places to hold all kinds of people in all manner of conditions.

The golden rule is 'Like attracts like'. Those of a similar nature inhabit the same spheres of existence, broadly speaking. And I've learned that no one can ever possess someone else.

This particular earth-bound entity — bound to the earth conditions by her jealous and vengeful nature — had been taken away by unseen friends, but not before the lessons had been learned by all. As soon as Marie gained her composure, she stopped emitting her violent psychic energies which allowed this visitation to take place. Once she had disciplined herself to remain calm when on her own at home instead of fearful, there was no further psychic activity.

And Marie never had another sleepless night after that.

4

The Angel of Death

Unemployment was high and work was difficult to get in those depression years of the 1970s. So, by now, I'd had an endless selection of really boring jobs. I'd walked the town as a kind of Council Planning Department 'spy', checking on people's gardens, roofs and sheds to see if they'd had permission to build. And I'd been in the Personnel Department at the British Steel Corporation. I was so unbelievably bored by that one that I complained to the manager of the whole multi-million pound complex.

'Just bring a book in to read,' he said. Well, you could have knocked me down with a feather. 'Little wonder this country's on the floor,' I thought to myself. There were other jobs too, all terribly unfulfilling and lacking any job satisfaction.

I guess it was then I decided I should apply for a place at college. It was better than being unemployed, and I'd thoroughly enjoyed all the plays and concerts I'd performed in at the amateur theatre groups in the YMCA.

So I knuckled down to learning a few speeches, one from Shakespeare — 'Romeo' no less! — and wrote away for an audition at the Welsh College of Music and Drama, Cardiff. I got the interview and on the morning of it I lost my way through Cardiff, being mis-directed by several people. So I was late arriving at the Principal's office.

I forgot my words, too — my mind just went completely blank! It was a disaster really, yet as I was glumly opening the study door to leave, the Principal called out, 'I'm prepared to accept you as a student. Not on what I've seen here today, but on what I've heard about you from references people have sent.' I should have been pleased I suppose, but I'm afraid I wasn't impressed.

College life was active and full of hard work. But there was one snag — I wasn't offered a Mandatory grant; instead they gave me a Gratuity grant, which was not much money and I was forever left short. My mother knew this and came to the rescue. She'd slip me back a few pounds out of the weekly grant money I'd been told to give her by Dad. 'Don't let him know,' she'd whisper. 'Put it in your pocket quickly.'

Dad most certainly did not approve of me attending College. Being there, however, taught me how to speak correctly and project my voice, how to move and dance well, and above all it helped me gain a certain confidence when appearing before audiences — something I would be grateful for in the years ahead.

Although I enjoyed the work, I was struck by the unreality of it all. It was make-believe, unreal, and had little connection with everyday life. I was also struck by the sudden shock of learning to be a traveller. I commuted two hours a day, 700 miles a week on dear old British Rail. I couldn't begin to count the number of times I've heard over their tannoy systems: 'British Rail regret the late arrival of . . .' As I stood on freezing-cold platforms deep in mid-winter, I often wondered, 'Do they really mean it?'

But unknown to me then, this was all training which was preparing me for some greater purpose in the days to come.

Life moved along slowly, but smoothly, until one day our front door burst open.

'Quick!' snapped my brother. 'The baby's on the way!'

Breathless, we dashed out into the car and sped through the town to Mount Pleasant Hospital, where my sister-in-law was in labour. Poor John didn't know what to do with himself. He paced backwards and forwards, to and fro, to and fro.

'You'll wear that lino out,' I quipped, but he took no notice. From inside one of the labour rooms, we heard a baby screaming the roof down.

'That's it!' I chirped. 'I'll bet you that's yours!' He wouldn't believe me, but I was right. His daughter, Claire, had been born. She'd given my sister-in-law a bad time, for she weighed over 10lbs at birth. John mopped the beads of sweat off his brow, glad it was all over and completely unable to believe their beautiful, chubby baby was a girl. He was extremely happy, but a shade disappointed, I think. Being a football fanatic and a player, he'd secretly hoped for a boy to follow his lead.

My mother was over the moon! At last she had the little daughter she'd always wanted. The fact she was a *grand*-daughter made no difference to her at all! She was overjoyed.

Then, within 18 months, we were back at the hospital again. But this time the powerful, screaming lungs belonged to my nephew, Johnathan.

My mother revelled in the new arrivals. She pampered them and nursed them in the family Welsh shawl that John and I were wrapped in as babies. And she completely spoiled them — as all Nanas do. Every weekend we'd see the children at our home, or we'd visit them at theirs. My mother was particularly close to Claire, the first, and when Claire began to cut her teeth by rubbing her gums wildly on the bridge of my mother's nose, she nicknamed her 'Mad Maggie'.

It was a joy to see them playing together. And of course, I was in my element, loving children as I do.

As soon as the weather broke, all of us except Dad drove up to Tredegar where my mother's parents lived, and four family generations were united under one roof. Nana and Grancha Price, their children, their grandchildren and their great-grandchildren. What a smashing day that was, seeing all those happy smiling faces. And my mother couldn't get enough of her special playmates. She worshipped them. Somehow, they'd brought a glow to her eyes, a new purpose to her life.

Everything seemed wonderful with the arrival of the babies, but life has its own unusual way of turning and changing. Soon, there was to be a dark cloud hanging over our happy family. A cloud that would abruptly end my childhood and violently throw me into loneliness and utter desolation.

I'm not given to superstition, but one winter's night I recall Uncle Billy and I were both reading quietly when a landscape picture loosed itself from the wall and plummeted down onto a shelf with a crash. Then the nail which held it bounced off the shelf and landed in my lap. Uncle Billy and I exchanged looks.

'Who put that picture up?' he queried.

'My mother did.'

'Well, there's trouble coming when a picture falls,' said Billy.

'Oh, don't be so superstitious,' I admonished. 'That's just an old wives' tale.'

'You listen to me, brother. The same thing happened not long before my mother took ill.'

I shrugged him off, clicking my disapproval. But indeed, those invisible hands which released the picture knew what they were doing, for shortly afterwards, my mother became unwell.

She'd had a good deal of trouble in the mornings for years with her stomach, and frequently she would feel sickly and out of balance. But this was something else.

She went for medical tests because she was in discomfort. Her energy was ebbing away and she was gradually losing weight. We all were quite worried about her. As soon as the results came through, she was rushed to the hospital to undergo stomach surgery. It was scheduled for the next day, and there was nothing we could do until the next evening when the operation would be over.

'We'll all be thinking of you, Mam,' I assured her with a kiss.

'I know you will, Stephen,' she drowsily returned, 'you're a good lad . . . a good lad . . . ' and she drifted into sleep.

The next day, Jayne, a friend, suggested visiting a fortune-teller she'd heard of — 'just for a laugh'. So I agreed, but at the appointed time Jayne backed out and I was left there on my own. Nevertheless, something told me I should go in. So I did.

The old lady led me through a dark, shabby passageway into a small, dirty kitchen. I remember thinking it was very similar to old Gran King's house, all those years ago when I was a boy. Everything there was awry and the smell of the fire filled the room. The mats were worn through, and as for the fortune-teller — well, she was about 60, with greasy skin and the features of a freshly-ploughed field. But there was some sort of goodness about her which checked my desire to leave. I didn't know what I was doing there anyway.

'Take no notice of the place, dear,' she croaked. 'Cut the cards.' I obeyed, and watched her crinkled hands shuffling the pack. Then there followed a string of confusing questions. She was so incredibly wrong, I felt like getting up and leaving, until she said: 'Someone isn't very well. Am I right?'

My ears pricked up but I was careful not to feed her any information.

'Well, love, whoever it is, you'll remember this year as their last one — the year they began to crack up.'

I walked out into the cold night air, troubled by that last statement. And it wasn't long before my father revealed to me my mother's true condition, as told him by the surgeons.

'Your mother has cancer,' he said.

When I could find the words, I broke the awesome silence with: 'She must have no pain, Dad . . . she mustn't have any pain . . .'

After this, I visited the hospital every day. The surgeons had discovered widespread cancer tissue throughout her body. She had been cut almost in two to check the growths, but nothing could be done for her. On the night of her operation I'd walked the three miles in pouring rain just to see her. Dad wouldn't drive me there because he reckoned she would still be under the anaesthetic. But I was not deterred.

When I arrived, the Sister-in-Charge refused me permission to enter. But when she went, I crept quietly unseen into mother's side-room. I moved apprehensively towards the bed. She had been propped up on one side, her back facing me. She lay there motionless, looking so frail that my eyes filled up with emotion. Slowly approaching her, I kissed her shoulder as a kind of healing gesture I guess, but she couldn't sense anything. She was unconscious, avoiding the desperate pain.

While she recovered the following day, Jayne and I went knocking on doors, collecting money for cancer research. And when I told my mother that night, she agreed it was a very good cause and gave a sad, knowing smile.

The doctors released her from hospital, but she was still very weak and painfully thin. The operation had been so extensive that she couldn't stand up straight. She walked very slowly and hesitatingly, with shoulders bowed over — the scar tissue pulling at the stomach and back.

It was agony to watch her suffering, this woman who was the centre of our lives. We all wondered how on earth she could manage to place one foot in front of the other. I used to hug her, and walk with her around the house.

Of an evening, when we were alone together by the fireside I would sit by her feet while she read her newspaper and completed the crosswords she loved. I asked her at such a time: 'Mam, what ambitions have you?' Her answer was as touching as her look.

'I've lived out all my ambitions, Stephen. I wanted a family and a comfortable home. I've two fine boys and my life is now complete.'

I couldn't answer her, for I was aware in that moment that, beyond any doubt, she knew her life was coming to a close.

As the days passed, she became weaker and weaker. Yet despite this, one day I found her carrying two heavy shopping-bags up the hill towards home. That was my mother — a fighter, a determined loving woman who never mentioned or grumbled about the agony she quietly bore without complaint.

As the weeks moved forward, she had to take to her bed. Unable to walk by now, she could barely move without pain.

One night she asked me for a pair of socks to keep her feet warm so I found the thickest I had and pulled back the sheets to put them on her. It was all I could manage not to show my shock. The bones of her feet were protruding, she'd lost so much weight. And when she asked me to rub her back to relieve the pain, I knew she wanted me to realize she was dying. Every bone in her spine almost stuck through her flesh — like knuckles on a hand.

She would sit on the side of the bed, counting the hours on the floor with her fingers to the next time the nurse would give a pain-killing injection. Then she decided to not to take any more medication, because it was blurring her last precious memories of us all. Although it was a brave and noble step to take, she simply had to reverse it, for the suffering was too great.

At night, I'd lie awake for hours in the next bedroom, listening for any sound of distress that might come from her. Secretly I'd cry and pray: 'Please God, give *me* the cancer and make her well again. *I'll* die,' I said, 'but please let her live. She's a good woman, a wonderful person. Please take me instead,' I would silently plead. But of course, I didn't realize in my youth that the Great Spirit of Life doesn't work that way.

Neither did I know that my father had been found crying at work. Poor Dad just couldn't understand why this was happening. My brother was also deeply hurt, but never spoke about his feelings. 'There's nothing we can do,' he'd say sadly.

As for me, I managed to contain my emotions until one evening at college. A brass band was playing Christmas carols and the music stirred my soul. Tears started to stream down my face as I left the crowded hall of students, all staring at me. Sally knocked at the cloakroom door.

'Are you all right, Stephen?' she asked. I couldn't find any words. I was sobbing uncontrollably; I was going to lose my mother. Knocking again, Sally called out: 'Stephen, is there anything I can do?'

'There's nothing *anyone* can do,' I said. 'That's the trouble.'

Now my mother's last days were approaching. Her family

drove down from Tredegar to be with her. She'd held my father and called out for them in delirium, knowing her time was almost spent.

It was Saturday night, and her breathing was very irregular. You could count the pauses between the breaths she took, and as the night progressed it became obvious that the lapses were getting longer.

By morning, I instinctively knew this would be her last day. Outside there was brilliant sunshine and I remember thinking, 'Why is the sun shining so brightly when my mother is dying?'

Inside, there was a heaviness all about the house. It was filled with silent moments when no one really felt like saying much. We didn't know what to say anyway.

About two o'clock, I climbed the stairs for the hundredth time to see her. She was lying motionless in the bed, eyes half closed, breathing whenever she could find the strength. I stood by the bedside and leaned over her and kissed her forehead.

'Good night. God bless,' I said, even though it was daytime. 'This is Stephen, Mam. Never forget I love you with all my heart.'

And in a whispering, almost inaudible voice, she replied: 'Stephen . . . I'm dying . . . ' I couldn't speak a word . . .

In a timeless daze, I pulled on my coat and walked down the hill to my mother's dearest friend and neighbour, Florrie. I entered Florrie's open door, but my vision was blurred by a wall of tears filling my eyes. I could barely form a sentence, but somehow managed to whisper: 'Mam's dying . . . if you want to see her please come up with me, I don't think she'll last the hour . . . '

In the stillness, Florrie put on her coat and together we walked up the hill. I don't know if we spoke much at all. Through tears I think Florrie said she was sorry, but I'm not altogether sure. I only knew I was numb and silent.

I climbed the stairs and Florrie sat down by the fire, content just to be there with some of my mother's other friends who had gathered for the end. Up in the bedroom, my brother and I closed in around the bed. My sister-in-law came inside and we stood silently, watching my mother's last few moments of life. We never said a word. My father, too upset to face the end, had gone next door to a neighbour.

The seconds ticked away and the memories flooded into my mind. Thoughts of our childhood filled my vision. Those happy picnics by the sea, the loving kindness my mother had shown to all the elderly folk in our street. I could see the time she collected me at the school when I was but a boy, but the other children were soaked in the rain because their mothers were nowhere in sight. And I recalled the wonderful moments we'd shared through our lives; and her gentle voice as she sat me upon her knee when I was just a lad and said, 'Stephen, I love you, son.' A million thoughts occured at once, a million kindnesses, thousands of loving moments. Then the bedroom came back into focus . . .

Her breathing was now very spasmodic. There were long pauses of utter silence. And then . . . My sister-in-law suddenly burst into tears, and my brother joined her. She had been counting the seconds between the pauses, and the last breath had gone . . .

It was all over . . .

My mother was dead.

John left wiping the tears from his eyes and I followed him to the bathroom, and we held each other tightly and cried from the very depths of our beings. A great dark cloud filled every corner of my mind as John and I sobbed and cried and clasped each other, heavy with grief and total despair. The sound of our tears echoed around the bathroom walls as the devastating fact of my mother's death struck home, right to the heart.

When my failing strength partly returned, I wandered through to the bedroom again, still unable to comprehend why we had suffered such a tragic loss, and I found Mary — one of my mother's friends — standing over her, fingering some rosary beads and praying for the safe-keeping of her soul, in a whispered, hushed voice that turned the room into the hallowed ground of a thousand souls in reverent prayer. Unable to watch any more, I slowly turned and wiped my eyes, and descended the stairs. It was three o'clock.

Florrie joined our tears; Mrs Ross could find no words to express her deepest feelings; then Nora from next door came through; and I just sat by the fireside, deep in my solemn thoughts.

All our lives had now come to an end. The light of my mother's smile had gone. The centre of our family had been taken from among us; the woman I loved had died.

How could life go on without her?

We'd lost our first, our last, our everything.

We'd lost our best friend.

We had lost our mother.

5

Revelation

On the morning after my mother passed, I was the first to rise. Drowsily, I crept into her room where her body lay motionless in death. I kissed her on the forehead and said: 'You were a marvellous person, and a wonderful mother.' And I left the room as silently as I'd entered it . . .

On the day of the funeral, I answered the door to the florist delivering wreaths and moving tributes. Only when the flowers were arriving did I fully realize that my mother had really died. I suppose it was some kind of delayed shock and I was quiet for most of those early hours. This was the first time I'd witnessed death so close at hand and it was a great, devastating blow to us all.

One by one, people began to gather in our living-room. Some were crying, others downcast and very solemn. They'd come to pay their respects to a much-loved woman. The door opened and a clergyman arrived. I didn't know him. I don't think any of us did, for we were not at all religiously minded as a family and followed no particular faith. If I'd had my own way, I wouldn't have had any outsiders in this special ceremony. As young as I was, I'd have taken it myself. But that wasn't the 'proper' way, and so they hired a clergyman to preside.

He started speaking empty, meaningless words. He had never even known my mother, so how could he possibly appreciate the loss she was to this world? My mother's sisters started to weep, so I placed my hand on one of their shoulders, squeezing it gently. Her tears moved me and my eyes filled up. Then a small voice somewhere inside my head said: 'Be brave. Try to be brave.'

The tributes were loaded into the hearse outside. There was one from all the children of our estate, another from the children of the school where Mam had worked as a playground supervisor. Soon, the hearse was so full of flowers the coffin could barely be seen. But right on the top of it was my own special tribute to her — a single red rose, placed in its own see-through box. And the card inside read: 'As long as *I* live, you'll never die.'

At the crematorium, I dimly recall that clergyman speaking more uncomforting words, while I kept my eye on the coffin as it slowly sank down at the side of his pulpit. He looked at me staring at it. And I remember thinking, 'That's the last I'll see of her now.' The service concluded and we sadly filed outside . . .

Someone asked me afterwards where I would like the ashes scattered, so I pointed out a small tree.

From this moment on, our family seemed to break apart. My brother got on with his life, father immersed himself in work and I tried not to think about what had happened. I dashed about filling my time with anything and everything to obliterate the sense of loss, not wanting to face the fact I'd never see my mother again. I comforted myself by thinking she was now at peace in 'heaven', although I didn't understand what that meant. All I knew was she was out of any pain, and I was grateful for that.

Dad and I were now under great emotional stress and our relationship, predictably, had quickly broken down. We were both exceptionally tense and terse, both missing Mam and neither of us mentioning it. The rift between us got so bad that one night his temper exploded and I got the worst of it as he slammed the door and went to bed in a rage. I sat alone, crying, sobbing, thinking to myself: 'He never would have done this if she were alive.' I was a deeply sensitive 20-year-old.

Life went on aimlessly from day to day. It seemed meaningless. Birth; life; death? What was the point of it all? I couldn't fathom any answers and nothing could soothe my spirit. To make matters worse, my college grant had run out and I was penniless. There were three weeks of graduation term left and I couldn't attend unless I found the £15 rail fare from somewhere. Even if I could raise it, I still wouldn't have any money for daily food. I was at my wit's end.

One afternoon, I found myself spilling the whole tale out to my brother. And, although he couldn't help because he was in financial difficulties himself, he did mention an endowment policy my mother had taken out for me years previously. 'It matures soon,' he informed me. 'Why not take it out now? You'll get about £16.'

That was the answer! After all, it's what my mother would have done. But when I approached Dad, he refused point-blank to release the policy. Desperate, I sought out the insurance company, clutching my identification details, and explained my precarious position.

'I'm sorry,' they said grimly, 'but we can't pay it out without your father's signature.' My heart sank. Now I'd have to go back and confront my father. So, swallowing my pride, I did.

But he wouldn't sign, and I was left completely in limbo.

The next day, Marion — Florrie's daughter — approached me stealthily. 'Look, I want you to take this £15,' she said, handing me a sealed envelope. 'Never mind how I borrowed it, get yourself to College. It would be your mother's last wish.' I was speechless, but from somewhere got the words to thank her gratefully and assured her I would pay it back when I could.

So I continued my final studies and graduated with my College Diploma. But it was no great joy to receive it, not the way I'd been feeling.

Even when the children came to call, it was not the same without their Nana there to greet them. Although Claire was only two she missed my mother greatly. She'd suddenly stop giggling in the garden and quite seriously ask: 'Uncle Stephen, where's Nanny O'Brien?' I hoped she hadn't seen my reaction.

What could I say? What could I tell this little girl she had loved so much? I framed my words gently.

'Nanny O'Brien's in heaven,' I told her. Claire became pensive for a few moments. Then followed up with: 'Is God looking after her, Uncle Stephen?'

'Oh, yes,' I said. 'God loved her so much, He's taken her to be near Him.' And then in the innocence of childhood, she wanted to know: 'Will I ever see her again?'

I took a breath. 'Oh, yes,' I said. 'One day I'm sure we'll all be back together again.' At least that was what I'd hoped, but I didn't really know.

Children have a strange way of putting their fingers right on the pulse of things.

One morning, something odd happened. Deep inside myself I knew I should visit my grandparents. It was as though somewhere in my soul, they were calling me, thinking of me. Perhaps the three of us were united in our grief, I don't know. But I did know I had to go to them. So I packed a bag and made for Tredegar, where they lived.

As the bus chugged and spluttered up the winding hillside roads, I couldn't help hearing my brother's laughter as we both joked and played childish games of 'I spy' with my mother on the same journey we had made so many times before. But now the seats beside me were empty, and another bump in the road broke my reverie.

Outside the sun was shining like a bright ball of fire in the sky, but the cold March air took my breath away as I approached my grandparents' home. Everything looked just the same from the outside; the creaky garden gate, the lace curtains at the window, the warmth that seemed to radiate around the very walls themselves.

As I walked up the path to the door, I passed the yellow goldenrods and remembered collecting bunches of them when I was no bigger than a sparrow, to present to my mother one Easter. Deep in my memories, I moved to the back of the house and knocked the kitchen door. How would they be feeling now, so soon after the funeral? What on earth could I say to them? I was so young. And secretly I hoped they wouldn't be shocked to see me, for I hadn't told them I was coming. But there was nothing to worry about. The door opened and I fell into my grandmother's arms.

'What a lovely surprise,' she said, smoothing the back of my hair and holding me tight. 'It's so good to see you, Stephen.' Grancha gave me a hug too, but he was still so very deeply hurt. I could see it in his solemn eyes.

Nana and Grancha were both in their 70's now and both utterly devastated by their eldest daughter's death. Quietly, we sat and talked together.

'God knows, it shouldn't have happened,' said my grandmother. 'We never expected one of our own to go first. It should have been one of us,' she said, stricken with grief. Grancha was still dumbfounded. Not a man of many words at the best of times, now he was walking around like a zombie. I can only dimly recollect him saying, 'She was only 49.' And he heaved a sigh of bitter regret.

As I listened, my eyes took in the humble room. Their house was just as I'd always remembered it, and the memories flooding back brought a lump to my throat. Then something inside me urged me to help Nana and Grancha in some way. I wondered what my mother would have done had she been there on that day — and my mind was made up.

I rolled up my sleeves, got a mop and bucket and a hoover, and cleaned the house from top to bottom until it shone like a new pin. You could see the reflection of your face in the lino after I'd finished this mammoth job. My mother often did this cleaning for them, and now it was my turn. Grancha kept saying: 'You needn't bother you know, Stephen.' But I think he knew why I did it.

After tea, I strolled out onto the mountains, those lovely hills and vales in the Welsh Valley. The grass was strong, the air crisp and clear, and I was totally alone with my memories. In the distance I could see the Nine Arches where we'd all picnicked when I was a lad. I walked past the weir, and in my mind's eye I could still see the children splashing happily in the waters.

All around me were the scenes of my mother's childhood, the things that made her the good person she was. But I couldn't remain on the hills, as much as I felt I wanted to. The sun was sinking and I ended my daydream and went to collect my travelling bag, my mind still full of those days of long ago.

As I bid my grandparents goodbye at the bus station, I said: 'I'll still come and see you both.'

'We know you will, boy,' replied Grancha, blinking back his tears. 'You do your best now to get on with your father, Stephen. You've only got each other now, you know.' And he hugged me. I got aboard the bus as he said: 'And never forget, we loved your mother more than words can say.'

The big bus pulled out of the station as I watched my grandparents disappearing from view through the back window. I was going back home, and I didn't want to go . . .

My nights were long and sleepless, my days empty and devoid of all love and kindness. People felt awkward in my presence, not quite knowing what to say or do. And Dad and I just couldn't communicate at all. If we spoke we'd just start another pointless argument. I didn't want to be harassed and condemned by every other word, but that's what was happening. So, when he came in, I went out; in this way, much difficulty was avoided, though when I couldn't time my departure right another awful session of being criticized would get under way. What terrible memories I have of these, my darkest hours.

Seeking some solace, I decided to sort through my mother's things. I felt impressed to do so, and it's a good job I did because soon afterwards items started 'walking' out of the house. Bit by bit our home was being taken away, until my father put a stop to it.

Up in the bedroom, I sifted through all the papers, photographs and jewellery my mother had collected over the years. There was nothing of any great value there; it was all inexpensive and sparkly — we never had much money at all to waste on the so-called finer things of life. I did come across my mother's wedding ring though, and decided I would keep it in memory of her.

I found snapshots of us all when we were youngsters. Those days seemed so far away now, somewhere in a distant past. Amongst the bundles I discovered birthday cards sent by my mother to John and me when we were infants. I sat on the bed fondling these treasured memories and was greatly moved when I read upon a card:

'To my darling Stephen on your first birthday.'

And there were kisses all along the bottom, and under them were the words: 'With all my love, Mam and Dad.' But Dad never sent cards, and the writing was my mother's.

That old feeling began haunting me again; that sensation of 'being in the world, but not of it'. Coupled with this, I felt so alone. My soul was touched as I came across a small heart locket. I had never seen it before. And when I opened it there was a picture of me on one side and my brother on the other, both as small boys. I still have it today.

The days rolled onwards and I began to feel unwell. I was losing weight. I wasn't eating properly and my nervous system couldn't cope with the strain on my resources. It was hard to climb the hill to our house, and I couldn't manage it without a few rests on the way. Mrs Walker asked me what was wrong when she found me sitting on the wall.

'Oh, nothing,' I returned, 'I just need to catch my breath.' My appearance was slowly changing. I'd lost such weight on my face that I began to look sunken and drawn. Florrie told me to take care of myself and get at least one decent meal a day. I don't think Dad paid much attention, and probably didn't even notice. But I just couldn't be bothered to buy food or prepare it.

This new way of life thrust upon us all had taken its toll of the whole family. The dark cloud it brought about us filled our lives with uncertainty and a nagging grief which pulled us all down into despair.

But somewhere out in the worlds of light beyond this grey little planet a soul was stirring. Through the mists of death the mighty power of love was planning to claim its own. . .

One evening, about three months after my mother died, I returned home on a late summer's night. Realizing the house was empty, I opened the door and suddenly heard my name called from above. I swung round, startled, and there in a brilliant blaze of light at the top of our stairs I saw my mother. She was beckoning and calling to me.

'Stephen! Stephen!' she cried out anxiously, 'Come up! Come up!' And she waved her hand for me to join her. Spellbound and light-headed, I turned on the hall light. I couldn't believe what I was seeing. How could this be?

'Stephen! Come up!' she called out once more, and she turned and moved out of my sight around the landing.

Dumbfounded and bewildered, I climbed the stairs at her command, looking around excitedly to see her. And when I reached the top of the landing, I heard her call to me again: 'Stephen!' Her voice was full of urgency.

I quickly swivelled to face the direction of the sound, and there was my mother again, standing outside my bedroom door, as large as life, bathed in glowing light. I stepped backwards, bracing myself against the wall. I didn't know what to make of this. I wasn't frightened, she was my mother. How could any son fear his mother's love? But how could she be here? She was dead. I'd been there when she took her last breath.

Yet here she was, standing before me, wearing a hospital robe and leaning on a walking-stick for support. She was still bowed over as I remembered her in her last days.

But those eyes, that face. It was my mother.

Slowly moving towards me, still smiling, she leaned forward and kissed me on the left side of my face, just as I had often done to her, and then she turned and laughed. It was that special laugh that only she could make. A laugh that said: 'I'm alive, what are you all worrying about?'

Then as I stared fixedly at her, mystified by it all, she faded from my sight. The landing suddenly lost its radiance, and I stood there totally alone. I don't know how long I stayed anchored to that spot. I just remember feeling dazed and perplexed as I eventually moved down the stairs, one step at a time, supporting myself on the walls as I went. I made my way to the living-room and sat on our settee, gazing across at my mother's chair. It was empty now. But I had just seen her. She'd spoken to me, called out my name from beyond death.

Slowly, gradually, a realization began to dawn. Somehow, through the power of our Love, she had returned. She had bridged that Great Divide and spoken to her son. She wasn't dead — she was alive! I had seen her!

But what should I do now? Should I tell the rest of the family? Surely they had a right to know? But how could I approach them with this news? The excitement made me dizzy, but I made up my mind I would tell them. I'd have to pick the right moment though. Right now, I just felt like dancing and shouting from the hilltops. I kept thinking to myself: 'If *she's* alive, then *everyone* lives. I must tell the world.'

When my brother called for coffee, the time was right.

'She's alive in another world,' I said.

John was confused and a little angry.

'She's dead, Steve. You *want* to see these things. Face the facts — she's gone. Our mother's dead.' I protested, but it was just no use. Yet, for her sake, I had to tell them all. That's what she would want me to do.

I shall never forget my father's face and the strange, fiery look in his eyes when I told him.

'Why you?' he snarled at me. 'If your mother came back, she'd come to *me* — not you. You're only her son, I'm her husband.'

'But I've told you the truth, Dad,' I said. 'I saw her.'

'She's dead son. You were at the crematorium. She's gone and she'll never come back. Your mother's *dead*.'

No one would believe me. Did they think I was lying? Why didn't they believe me?

Sad and angry, I walked out through the fine rain and eventually wandered into an old Catholic church. It was completely empty so I approached the altar, still deep in thought and consternation. The atmosphere was so peaceful, so tangible you could almost grasp the tranquillity. Moving towards the altar I noticed a candle-stand, and upon it was the inscription:

I HAVE SUFFERED.

I don't know why I did it, but I took a nearby candle and lit it, and placed it in the centre of the stand — for my mother.

Then I found myself sending out a prayer. Quietly I whispered: 'I tried to tell them, Mam. I tried but they wouldn't believe me. *I* know you're alive, even if no one else wants to accept that. I did my best for you,' I said.

Noiselessly, I sat at one of the front pews and became very still, thinking of how wonderful she had been to us all in life, and how saddened she must be to think only I accepted her existence beyond death.

Just then, a hand touched my shoulder. Beside me was a pleasant young priest in full ceremonial garb.

'Are you alright, son?' he asked. 'Do you need any help?'

'Oh, no thank you,' I said, 'I just thought I'd sit here quietly and meditate — if that's all right.'

'Of course,' he smiled. 'You take as long as you like, son.' And he turned to go back up the aisle, fading away into thin air as he went . . .

6

The Mission Begins

Although no one believed that my mother had visited me from beyond death, I knew what I'd experienced. Somehow, somewhere, she still lived and existed as herself. I never doubted my sanity — no one is more practical than me. So, I now resolved to keep quiet about it, and do my best to get on with building a new life.

I got a job as an Assistant Stage-Manager at a theatre, but the contract only lasted eight weeks and it was unstimulating work. However, there were some memorable moments. Like the time I authorized the curtain to be raised too early during a deadly-serious drama, only to reveal a workman dashing panic-stricken off the set. The audience hooted at my mistake. Or the comedy football match held for local charity. They dressed me up as a frightened goalkeeper, and every time the ball came near the nets, I'd run behind them and cower on the ground! Everyone wore fancy-dress costumes and one of our team was hilariously funny. She'd dressed as a tipsy Christmas Fairy, complete with stiffened tutu and sparkling wand. Whenever she kicked the ball, she collapsed to the ground, spread-eagled and unconscious, and she had to be carried off by two clown stretcher-bearers! The crowd really loved her!

Back at the theatre, at odd moments during the performances while I stood in the silent wings, my mind would fill again with visions of my mother's spirit-return. I'd shrug my shoulders, and get on with the job, fearful of making any more silly mistakes.

After the contract ran out, I forced myself into travelling to several auditions — something I didn't want to do. I'd go hither and thither, mostly to London, at great expense and with no luck whatsoever. It was a degrading experience, being auditioned: they lined people up like 'prize cows' being paraded, judged and — nine times out of ten — rejected.

Then, a very peculiar thing happened. As most of the important events in my life seem to do, sudden changes occured literally overnight. One morning I woke up and announced to the fresh air: 'That's the end of that.' And I really said it with vigour and meant it. With positive determination, I instantly knew that my days with the theatre were over. I was tired of make-believe, bored with portraying someone else. I wanted to be *me*, Stephen O'Brien, the real person inside. I'd suddenly thrown off an old overcoat and now I was setting out on a new tack. I don't know why this decision happened so quickly and with such sudden certitude, but it did. It was as though I wanted to move forward into a new area of being, a new way of life. And quite unknown to me, that's exactly what was about to happen.

One evening while ambling through the town, I realized I was close to a Spiritualist church. It was old Gran King's church — the one she'd spoken of all those years ago when I was 10. I turned the corner and saw the painted sign:

Oxford Street Spiritualist National Union Church.

As I neared it, I had a most remarkable experience. I felt as though I was as light as a feather, and just as though I was floating six inches above the pavement. It was an incredible sensation of levitation, and I remember thinking to myself, 'Someone wants me to go in here.' So I did.

Carefully, I tip-toed up the 20 steps to the inner door, behind which was an upper room. I stopped for a moment. Should I enter or not? What would I find inside? A thousand thoughts clamoured for my attention. Little did I know, but I was standing on the threshold of a completely new life. Once I crossed that doorway, my whole world would change — but I had no idea of it then.

What were the people in there whispering about? The muffled conversation floated past me. I took a deep breath, pushed open the door and went inside.

I was rather surprised to find a small horseshoe of chairs neatly arranged around a fire, and all heads turned and smiled at me. The people seemed quite 'normal'. Just then, a kindly, elderly lady beckoned to me. 'Good evening,' she said with a warm, smiling voice. 'Come and sit down. You're very welcome.' Gingerly, I took my seat opposite her.

'Been here before?' she asked.

'No,' I said, not even sure why I was there now.

This elderly lady, whom everyone called Mrs Palmer, stood up and announced the Open Circle was going to begin. 'Oh,' I thought, 'this is what Gran King used to talk about, where she gave messages out.' And that note of familiarity helped me to settle in.

They trembled their way through a hymn, unaccompanied, and Mrs Palmer delivered a beautiful, spontaneous prayer, sincerely given from the heart and very moving. She called for peace to come into the world through each individual soul and that brother should love brother. She embraced the whole of humanity with her thoughts, which made me feel quite at home, for these were my sentiments too.

Gradually, all tensions ebbed away, and without any hesitation Mrs Palmer began speaking to invisible people. She passed accurate messages on from them. I was completely enthralled. She saw 'dead' relatives and named them, and each person she singled out gratefully accepted their communications, delighted the medium could even tell them where their loved-ones had lived. Personal messages, factual messages and snippets of information flowed out to them, as I sat captivated. I couldn't take it all in at first, it was too marvellous for words.

But then, something happened. I became uneasy. All at once

I felt that unseen 'friend' of mine drawing close to me. I could feel him standing at my left hand side. His electric presence was so strong. For a few panicky moments I lost touch with my surroundings. I rubbed my eyes, and opened them wider to watch the rest of the meeting.

Mrs Palmer's voice brought me smartly back into the room. 'There's an Indian healing your back. Have you hurt it?' she asked. I nodded.

'Yes,' I replied, thinking that she could 'see' the person I was 'sensing'. And I wondered if my mother would communicate. Was she even present in this church? Could she get a word through to me at all? But she didn't.

The medium mentioned the fireworks at home with Dad, detailing facts with pinpoint accuracy. And then she thanked me for my attention and promptly left me. A wave of disappointment swept over me. But then . . .

'Oh, a strange thing's occurred here; I'll come back to that young man, please. As I was going to leave you, I saw a woman's hand place one red rose across your lap.'

I went numb. I was speechless. What was that she said? One red rose? But I'd only ever given a red rose to one person in my whole life — that special rose in its own see-through box I'd presented to my mother at her funeral.

'Can you understand that?' Mrs Palmer questioned. But there was a pause. My mind was momentarily stunned. 'Does that mean anything to you?' she asked again.

'Oh, yes,' I replied, 'It means a great deal to me.' And in that moment I knew my mother was with me.

I walked out of that church fully realizing why I'd danced on air when I'd approached it an hour earlier. Death's silence had once again been broken. She had communicated again and my joy was indescribable. I felt the whole world should know that a mother had returned from the eternal realms beyond the grave to speak with her son.

All week, I couldn't get that message out of my mind. I couldn't concentrate on a thing. My thoughts kept slipping back to Mrs Palmer and her vision. Through this complete stranger Mam had lovingly returned the flower I'd given her. And those other messages the medium gave had made such a powerful impression upon me. The moment I'd left the church, I knew I would return. But unfortunately work commitments wouldn't allow it for a few weeks.

Those weeks were endless, and I didn't tell a living soul about my visit to the church. I remembered their reaction last time.

Every fibre of my being drew me back to witness Mrs Palmer's mediumship again. And when I was at last able to make another visit, Mrs Palmer asked: 'Would you say an opening prayer for us?' I don't know why I said it, but I just said 'Yes', and was quite calm about the whole thing. I couldn't to this day tell you why, because I had never prayed in public before and I hadn't a clue what to say. Don't ask me where the words came from, but they were certainly not from me. They flowed as though some external intelligence had used my mind, blended with me to express itself. I didn't recognize the phrasing or the vocabulary, yet I couldn't stop the words flowing out. It was an unnerving experience.

Mrs Palmer was obviously impressed by the invocation judging by her subdued comments of 'Bless him' as it was delivered. Then after the next hymn, bravely trembled again without accompaniment, the service got underway.

But as much as I wanted to listen, I couldn't quite register anything properly. My mind kept performing quiet little spins, and it was impossible to keep my eyes open for very long. Pulling myself together, and hoping no one had seen my head tilt slightly to the side, I caught Mrs Palmer's voice saying: 'Have you anything to give out?' I was going to say 'No', but before I could form the word, five lightning-quick spirit messages rushed from my lips at incredible speed. They were all accepted by open-mouthed watchers. When I'd finished, I felt rather embarrassed, for there was a deathly hush in the room. Why were they all looking at me like that? Had I done something wrong? I didn't think so, for when I turned, Mrs

Palmer was positively beaming. I didn't know what I'd said, and what's more, I didn't know I was going to say it.

But the people seemed delighted with the evidence, after the initial shock had worn off. All of them were pleased, except one: a lady who'd received a prediction concerning an emotional shock that was about to happen. She was warned to brace herself in readiness, for her feet were about to be emotionally knocked from underneath her. She couldn't understand it, and neither could I. After all, I didn't give her the information, I simply received it and had it passed through me.

The following week, as I entered the church eager to do more mediumship, this woman whisked me off into a corner, gabbling her profuse thanks for the spirit-warning. She and her husband were buying a dream-house and as far as they were concerned everything was settled. But two days after the prediction, they'd been gazumped: someone had made a higher bid and they lost their house.

'If you hadn't given me that message,' she said, 'I'd have had a nervous breakdown.' I was shocked.

And so the first visible threads of the pattern began to slowly appear. Behind those earliest communications, no doubt delivered by my invisible 'friend', there was a hidden world at work. Behind the words that had rushed from my young and inexperienced lips, there was an intelligence, outside of my own, making its presence felt — and serving because it loved.

For 20 years, they'd stood at the doorway and knocked. At odd times, they had peered through the portal known as 'death' and reassured me, or realigned my footsteps back onto the pathway that had led me to discover an eternal life.

Now that doorway had been unlocked and flung open wide. At long last the connections had been made: I was now a medium.

7

The Coming of White Owl

Without doubt, the messages were reaching me from an external source, but what I didn't know was who was sending them.

Walking along the fresh seafront, kicking up the sand between my toes, I sent out requests wondering who was responsible. It was a puzzle I couldn't solve. Then, one evening, a young medium told me: 'Your guides want to speak with you. They say they can write through your hand. Take up the pen.' Well, anything's worth a try. So I set a time the next day and did as I was advised.

After a short period of silence, all at once I felt a powerful urge to write. Putting pen to paper, the words flooded through my mind and out through my hand. The speed at which I wrote amazed me; some of the words merging into a blur on the page. But the Other Side wasted no time in making itself known.

The writings were being given under the direction and supervision of my main Spirit Control. Could this be my 'friend' of long ago? Avidly, I scanned the pages and read:

I am your guiding soul. I am a part of you, and you are a part of me. Through all your trials and difficulties, I have travelled with you. Every tear you have shed, I have shed also. My love for you is higher than the mountains, deeper than the oceans. I am your Guardian Spirit. I am your Friend.

My name is White Owl.

I was deeply moved, and very eager to learn more of this man. He continued:

> When on earth I was a Red Indian, but I died at 21. My life was taken by a jealous man. He struck me with a tomahawk at the base of my skull and I fell lifeless into the river.

His story was gripping and in parts very soul-stirring. He went on to describe his life as a boy in his tribe and how at 14 he passed his man-task. They sent him out into the countryside and forests with no weapons or food and he had to survive. And when he returned to his people, he was proclaimed a man. He recalled his great love for his woman, Running Deer, whom he cherished deeply. He spoke about his days of courage and his youth when he rode like the wind on his white stallion, Silver Cloud.

This remarkable 'dead' man had been my companion before my birth, he claimed, and he was approached by Higher Minds to guide my footsteps along a spiritual pathway:

> I was told that there was much work to do back in the dark earth-world. I was approached by those who know to return and guide a spirit on earth who would be a medium between two worlds. That spirit is you, the soul. I was told where you would be born, who your parents would be and given all the necessary information about 100 years — as you would gauge time — before these events took place. I prepared for my mission, which I undertook gladly to help mankind towards a greater understanding of the Truth.

My breath was taken away. Slowly, but surely, everything began to crystallize. Those strange events of my childhood held some meaning at last. A thread of purpose was now visibly moving through them. The visions, the pathway, the predictions — they all seemed to fit into place as part of a great Scheme, worked out and set down before my birth, according to White Owl.

He further told me that there was much work before us both and that I would have to prepare myself for hardship and disappointment as well as the great satisfaction of knowing that fallen souls would be lifted back into the light:

> There is much darkness in your world. It is the darkness of ignorance of which I speak; that all-engulfing blackness that is keeping mankind from the great freedom which knowledge brings. Together we can help to dissipate that darkness and replace it with light. But I cannot do this alone, I need your help. In the earth-world you could be my voice, my hands and ears. If you can help me to achieve my mission, then when your day comes to join me here in the realms of light you will look back upon your life on earth and be well satisfied that you and I both will have helped to pave the way for greater peace on your small planet.
>
> I do not work alone in these tasks. Just as I am in touch with you, so there are those much more evolved than myself in touch with me. This chain of minds links high into the realms of spirit, and down these connections teachings can pour into your world. But only if you are willing to co-operate with us. The pathway will not be easy; in fact, it will be difficult. But at the end of the road, it will have been worth while. This I can promise you.

He was asking for my unswerving co-operation. What could I answer? I was still young, still inexperienced as a medium. I didn't have a vast knowledge of anything, least of all life and its meaning. So I whispered out to him, 'Please give me some time to think about it. I'll give you an answer soon.'

His thanks were quick to be rendered. 'You will not regret it,' he said.

Several days passed by. Back down at the sea-front I wandered along the sandy shore and gazed out at the waves crashing in on the rocks. With each breaking wave I pondered on this 'mission' he had mentioned. And I wondered why I was the person he'd chosen to achieve it. My young mind wasn't capable then of perceiving the greater events to follow in the years lying, as yet, before me. Still, I reasoned, he must have known me well, if he had followed my progress through life for so long. And on the strength of this I knew he'd fully realize that when I gave my word on something the pact was sealed.

As the seagulls cried overhead and the sun gently sank beneath the ocean waters, I sat by the edge of the shore and quietly closed everything earthly out of my mind. Listening to the soft breeze and the lapping waves, I sent out my thoughts to this man who claimed guardianship of my work. And in those quiet moments he heard me say: 'Very well, I'll help you, my friend.'

'I am so grateful,' he returned, 'for now my mission begins.'

At every service after this, White Owl entranced me to deliver an inspired address, lasting from 15 to 45 minutes, to the people. The length and content depended upon their needs. I couldn't remember all he would say through me, but I taped the talks and learned much from listening to them over and over again. In this way we both became very close, both holding the same philosophical ideas and moral codes. Our use of language also showed similarities after a while. And as each psychic link took us forward, so our attunement became stronger.

Usually at public meetings a song was sung and I'd close my eyes, becoming very relaxed. I'd start to feel light-headed. Then my eyes would roll backwards as though they were viewing the inside of my dark head — that's how it felt anyway. Then my voice-box would start to move, an odd kind of pulling sensation as though someone was testing the mechanisms. At this point, I'd feel as though I was someone else. I can't really express that sensation very well. I suppose it was a feeling of being older, much wiser and more experienced about the vital things of life. White Owl has often described his link with me at such times thus:

It is a subtle blending of two minds, so closely joined that they appear to be one. Indeed, for those moments of attunement it is as though two personalities are functioning through one individual.

Imagine two tuning-forks both set at the same musical pitch. If you strike one it begins to resonate and vibrate the surrounding atmosphere, creating its own unique sound. But move it closely alongside its counterpart and you will find that the unstruck tuning-fork will begin to sing at the same pitch. It responds to the vibrations of its neighbour, both singing together because they are both naturally attuned to one another.

So it is with mediumship. The Spirit Control has to attune himself with his medium, and vice versa. Upon the precision of this at-one-ness rests the success of the experiment in communication.

He also gives an explanation of how he and I can blend our minds:

The medium has fields of energy about him; these are seen by us as pulsating light. I, too, have 'auras' such as these. We in Spirit exist at a much higher frequency or rate of vibration than you do on earth. When I wish to be beside my medium I firstly have to think myself close to him. By this act of concentrated and purposeful will, I descend from my higher world, lowering the frequency of my spirit body to approximate the frequency of the auras about my medium. When the two wavelengths are closely vibrating at roughly the same rate, attunement has taken place.

After this it sometimes can prove very difficult to retain this at-one-ness. There are many factors involved which can prevent attunement being held. Communicating from my side of life is not an easy process. It may look easy when it is working proficiently, but I can assure you it is not a simple matter.

When I am attuned to my medium a great many of my thoughts can pass through his mind. And thus I make myself heard in your world.

Although White Owl's public trance talks were most impressive, especially as at many of them he began with a blessing delivered in his own tongue, I still had some doubts as to the separateness of his identity. I was not an ignorant student of the paranormal. I was well read and above all I possessed a most analytical mind. It was these qualities which caused me deep concern about whether or not the trance talks were from the separate personality known as White Owl, or whether they could be springing from some deeper part of myself. Could they be what many researchers had called 'a secondary personality', a portion of the medium assuming a guide's character?

The largest obstacle against these theories was the content of the talks my guide delivered. Afterwards, I had to look up words he used to find out their meanings. Also, he spoke about matters which had hitherto not even entered my thinking. And if I was ignorant of them, how on earth could I speak so fluently and make such good common sense of subjects unknown to me? Nevertheless, I'm by no means a gullible person and I required further evidence, more proof. Naturally, White Owl must have been aware of this because it wasn't long in coming.

I possess that rare quality of losing touch with the room I'm in and experiencing my mind filling with scenes of the past and things which might have been — that day-dreaming quality which so many visually-active minds find natural. This was to prove beneficial, for it meant that under certain circumstances I could be taken from my physical body and astral-project. My mind could dissociate with its environment and in my spirit-body I could travel to locations in the spirit-realms. Such an experience is perfectly real, substantial and overwhelmingly convincing to any sceptic who may have tasted it. And I was about to do just that.

One day, while quietly meditating, I suddenly found myself loosed from the earth and I arrived in a plush, verdant valley. The colours were bright and intensely vibrant, far more *alive* than any we have here on earth. The very light about me was filled with life. And just a few yards away I could see a cascading waterfall, just like the one White Owl described to me in his writings. He would often bathe there with Running Deer, his woman. The water was gushing down and splashing with an unearthly musical sound. And there, just a few feet away from the stream, stood White Owl's white stallion, Silver Cloud. He was a magnificent horse. And there he was in all his beauty, champing at the grasses. His slim fetlocks looked as though they might hardly hold him erect, and yet I knew instinctively that with them he could race the wind.

Suddenly, he pricked up his ears and raised his quizzical eyes until he was staring right at me. He'd noticed I'd arrived. Then all at once, the scenes shifted rapidly and I was caught up in the embrace of White Owl. We stood together against a backdrop of purple-headed mountains.

His deep bronze skin, his well-shaped handsome features, and his hair — raven-black and billowing in the mountain breeze — this was such a real excursion. For the first time in my memory I looked into the eyes of this man who had been my unseen 'friend' all along my pathway. And in that moment I knew I was loved and cared for, not only by him, but by many others associated with him.

'It is I,' he said, and he smiled at me . . .

And in the next instant, I was sitting back in my armchair, feeling heavy and dull once again. The cold, grey earth all about me, so slow and uninteresting. It was an experience I'd never forget.

However, as wonderful as that excursion was, it was still something experienced only by me; a subjective happening. But White Owl must have known this too, for I was soon unexpectedly invited to attend a Transfiguration meeting with a well-known medium, Mrs Queenie Nixon. Quite by chance (?) a seat became available in a car going there. I took the opportunity, not even realizing what a Transfiguration meeting was. Mrs Nixon entered a trance state and her two main controls, Paul and Sister Edith, explained the whole procedure to the capacity crowd.

As we sat in the blacked-out hall, lit only by a small ruby lamp directed at Mrs Nixon's face, it became clear that her spirit guides were going to draw a special substance called ectoplasm from the people gathered and condense it around the medium's head. Then the spirit people would use it to make themselves visible. They would materialize their features using the medium's bone structure upon which to place their own 'mask'. I've since seen many mediums claiming this rare ability of physical mediumship, but none have measured up to the talents of Mrs Nixon.

In the black room, she called out a message for me which was acceptable and quite correct. Then, as Sister Edith put it, 'We're now going to try and bring your people to you.' As we all watched, the transformation was remarkable. Mrs Nixon did *not* pull her features and distort them as some charlatans or deluded folk would do; she *actually* transfigured.

First to arrive was my grandmother — Dad's mother — and without doubt it was most certainly her. The nose, the half-closed eye, the hair and the heavy jowls. It was Mary-Jane without any question. She disappeared by dematerializing and then next came my mother. She wasn't so successful as Mary-Jane, but nevertheless Mrs Nixon's hairstyle visibly changed, the cheekbones heightened, and my mother was reasonably recognizable. Paul, the guide, had already explained it wasn't easy for newcomers to the spirit-world to achieve success. But to clinch it all, my mother managed to whisper through a few words. Not many, but they were very evidential.

'Thank you for the flower,' she said. Reference again to that one special rose I'd given her at her funeral. Without a doubt she was present and doing her best to materialize.

It was not only *I* who saw her either; *everyone* could see these changes occurring around the medium. We'd already been treated to witnessing Mrs Nixon's hairline receding as a bald gentleman transfigured for his daughter in the hall, and we'd marvelled at the little girl who came through to her mother and how Mrs Nixon had changed from an elderly lady into a youngster complete with visible plaits in bows. So my mother's attempts were sympathetically received by all. A woman near to me said to her companion: 'Well, just look at that! It's a completely different person.'

My mother quietly said: 'Watch . . . watch.' And when she dematerialized, there was a short pause. We all waited to see what was coming. By now I was breathless, the whole experience having thrown me into a stunned condition. Yet I was quite able to hear the gasps from the audience as Mrs Nixon changed from an aged lady into a healthy, bronze-skinned young man. The features were exceptionally clear, the dignity shone from every pore. This spirit had the countenance of a highly compassionate soul. There, in that dark hall, I was gazing at the materialized face of my Guardian Spirit, White Owl. Without any doubt, here was the same man who had recently caught me up in his embrace on the mountain-tops on the Other Side. He was noble, and finely featured. I called out to him and he turned and looked me right in the eyes, picking out my exact location from amongst the 200 present in the blackness.

He didn't speak, he simply smiled. A dignified happy smile of knowing. He had achieved his goal. From beyond the veil he had used another being's exceptional mediumistic talents to prove his separate identity.

'Say something to him,' said a lady near me. 'Speak to him.' For a few uncertain moments I remained quiet. And when next his compassionate deep brown eyes met mine, I called out to him: 'It's lovely to see you again. I believe in you.'

And he smiled right back at me, and dematerialized.

8

Communications from Beyond

There were plenty of opportunities for service. I worked in a jeweller's by day and as a medium by night. Every Saturday I'd be at the Open Circle unfolding my powers under the expert tuition of Mrs Palmer. In those early days I couldn't get enough contact with the spirit-people to satisfy me. And each time I worked my abilities, they strengthened and the mediumship proved itself genuine; people kept coming back time and again to tell me the information checked out. Of course, there were 'misses' as well as 'hits', but gradually I got more proficient.

Then one day Mrs Palmer said: 'Stephen, you're ready to take a meeting on your own. How do you feel about that?'

Without any hestitation I replied, 'Fine.'

'You'll be all right,' she said. 'They've told me you're capable of it, and I've watched you working. You can do it.' And so the plan was set.

As the big day drew near, the announcement in the local paper advertised Mrs Palmer, but only we knew that it was I who would take the meeting in her place that coming Wednesday night.

All heads turned as I arrived at the church, and there were positive gasps as I went behind the curtain into the medium's rest area. Mrs Palmer straightened my tie — she was to chair for me — and we took the platform. I was announced as 'Young Stephen, a new medium.'

Soon the second hymn was being sung and all at once I felt

extremely nervous. Reaching for a glass of water, I could see my hand shaking uncontrollably. I couldn't stop it with my thoughts — then suddenly I felt the most unearthly peace descend upon me, just as though some wiser, elder being was blending with my mind. All my nervousness ceased; my hand became still; the shaking stopped, and I felt calm within. In that moment I had some conception of what the peace that passes all understanding may be like.

I rose to my feet, overshadowed by my inspirer who began to speak to the people. To this day, I can't recall what was said. the next thing I remember was sitting down and opening my eyes. Realizing I was seated, I was quickly about to stand again but Mrs Palmer beat me to my feet, announcing: 'Out of the mouths of babes has come forth wisdom.' I guess that meant it was understood and found to be meaningful.

Then the spirit messages flowed to me, through me, and were gratefully acknowledged. The words were precise, and the visions were crystal clear — I can even remember them today. Then, before I knew I'd started, I was called to time and had to sit down again. I'd spoken for an hour and a quarter and it seemed like just a few moments. Time, as we know it, was meaningless — it passed so swiftly when I was attuned to the Greater World and working with it.

After the meeting people came up to the platform to shake my hand and express their thanks for the service. I couldn't register it all fully, their words came at me ... 'Thank you for a lovely evening' ... 'Very evidential, Mr O'Brien' ... They'd obviously enjoyed it and it was nice to know I'd helped people. Afterwards, over a much-needed cup of tea, I sat awaiting Mrs Palmer's verdict. Hers was the opinion that really mattered the most. She smiled and congratulated me with: 'When can we book you again then?' And I knew I'd passed my first test.

The next week, a medium taking the meeting singled me out for a message. With tightly closed eyes, she pointed directly at me and proclaimed: 'The spirit-people would like to work with you to spread the knowledge of a life after death to the people.

Many are called but few are chosen.'

'Why me?' I kept asking myself. I didn't fully understand. When you're young, you can be right in the midst of important experiences and fail even to register them. But before I knew it I'd been recommended to all the churches in South Wales, and many took the opportunity to book my services and try me out.

Sundays used to be such boring days but now they were the most interesting days in the month. Every weekend, without fail, I travelled out to churches or halls to take public services. I did many midweek meetings too. The next few years were packed with unstinting service. I didn't have time to think! I was dashing about everywhere, serving wherever I could. I never refused a booking and everywhere I appeared I was asked to return. And I'd always attend when booked, even if I wasn't feeling well. I reckoned an appointment had been made with the spirit friends and I should respect that and not let them down.

Sometimes it was such a rush to reach a church. After working hard all day, I'd barely have time to wash and change before whizzing out. Yet they were happy days, full of laughter, learning, hard work and challenge. But I really didn't mind the difficulties too much because I did so enjoy delivering my mediumship, trying to help people by doing the best I could. At last I felt needed and capable of giving service to the community — and I was happy.

I served without thought of any reward, there was no charge, and I even paid my own expenses for travelling. If I was driven by anyone to a church then they would often refuse their petrol money, or put it back into the church building funds. And all the time I was growing, learning, developing as a person and as a medium. By doing the work, I slowly realized that 'dying' doesn't change the individual at all. They still cared . . .

Mrs Phyllis Fowler's father contacted her with the surprising news that she would go into hospital for tests. And although this was Christmas-time, he gave the dates 10–14 January. And she received her call from the hospital on 12 January — right in the middle!

Then I got the name Leo Atkins. He said he'd helped down-and-outs. 'Does she remember serving food to the vagrants in St Paul's Church crypt?' he asked. Mrs Fowler did. It was charity work she'd willingly undertaken. Mr Atkins mentioned his wife, still on earth, and her illness. Mrs Fowler knew of this. Then he told her: 'I've met my son and I'm with him in heaven.'

'Oh, I'm so glad,' she said. 'His son was found dead, suddenly, I think. Poor Mr Atkins was distraught because he loved the boy so much.'

Then, suddenly, a vagrant appeared before me. He tipped his battered hat and held out a coin in his toil-worn hand. 'Thank her for this,' he said. I did, and she recalled never passing him without giving him something from her purse. What a remarkable lesson for us all. He hadn't forgotten her kindness.

Then her father contacted again. 'We were with you last Wednesday night when you had your angina attack. You were alone and thought your time had come.' She had indeed, but she hadn't told a living soul about it. 'We were all around the bed,' he told her, 'your mother, Uncle Jack, your grandmother Ellen, and me.'

Then her beloved husband, Idris, made contact with her. 'March the 31st,' he said. And this was their Wedding Anniversary. He sent her all his love 'for nursing me through paralysis for $7\frac{1}{2}$ years before I died'. And she wiped a tear from her eyes. He'd also brought her Auntie Gladys with him, saying she'd died in childbirth. I could clearly see her lying in the coffin, both her arms entwined around her long, black shiny hair falling down to her waist.

Mrs Fowler was very grateful for her contacts. 'Don't thank *me*,' I said. 'Thank your family. They still love you greatly.'

I lost count of the times I helped psychic organizations out of difficulty. Perhaps on an afternoon I'd be relaxing and a voice would ask: 'Will you take a meeting tonight?' The place was then named. I'd dress up and as I'd walk through the door a frantic secretary would beg me to conduct the meeting because 'the medium hasn't turned up'. They could never understand why I wasn't flustered by the prospect.

At one such meeting, a 93-year-old woman was contacted by her father.

'He says you're not going over yet — there's work for you to do.'

'Oh, but I'm ready!' she gasped in surprise. But I had to report that Dad didn't want her Over There just yet. He identified himself by showing me the top of his little finger on his left hand was missing. 'A pig bit it off,' she reported.

Her Dad brought her reassuring evidence. He told her he'd followed her to St Anne's Hospital, where she thought she'd die but survived surgery. He said her mother, grandfather John and he would meet her when her time came to go across to the spirit-world. And he added joyfully, 'We'll have a wonderful shindig, and Auntie Annie'll play the piano.' Dad said they'd lived at 'the Parade', and a Mrs Irene Davis — their next door neighbour — returned along with Mr Harris, the butcher. She accepted them with a smile.

One of the funniest messages I gave was when I wanted to contact someone who knew a place called ' Pembridge Way'. I'd seen the street sign from the spirit world. An elderly woman claimed the link. Her father communicated, so I started the message by saying: 'Your Dad says someone is deaf but is too *vain* to wear a hearing aid.'

'Pardon?' she said, 'I didn't quite catch that.' The whole place erupted into laughter, people were holding each other at the thought of her father's clever way of putting his message across. I would never have embarrassed her like that, but I must admit it was very funny. The lady was the only one who didn't get the evidence!

Then there was the contact from an old lady in the spirit-world who returned to admonish her bewildered husband. She was furious because he'd buried her without her false teeth! Vain in life, death obviously hadn't changed her.

'I arrived without them!' she kept shouting. 'Tell him I'll clip him around the ear when he gets over here!' Of course, it was given in the spirit of love and the husband smiled, recollecting this was the kind of person she was.

There were touching communications too. Another recipient, Mrs Sylvia Jones was, at first, startled to receive her husband's name from the spirit-world. 'Dillwyn-John' communicated calling her 'Tiny'.

'That's my nickname,' she explained. He brought Jenny, her mother, along with him and also Aunt Ethel with her two adored Scottie dogs. 'I used to take them everywhere with me,' said the Aunt. Mrs Jones agreed.

There were some tearful moments when Dillwyn addressed his wife and daughter: 'I miss you both,' he said. And to his daughter he advised: 'Take care of your mother, she's one in a million.' The four of us were crying; Mrs Jones, her daughter, and Dillwyn in the spirit-world — and misty eyes from me.

It's moments like these that emphasized to me the sacred beauty of communication, and why it should ever be undertaken with the greatest of dignity and respect for the feelings of all parties involved. I watched many mediums working publicly, and quite frankly was extremely disappointed in them. Many of them were not even polite to the public. There is no excuse for this in my eyes.

Politeness is not only exhibited by the people of our world however. I well remember a tall, blonde airman appearing behind a gentleman seated in a crowd. This airman walked over to me, gave his name and shyly pulled at my trouser-leg, asking: 'Please would you give that man a message from me? I'd be very grateful.'

Not all communicators were so friendly. Like the step-father who returned to Mrs Donald. He identified himself by returning in a furious temper. As far as I can remember, he was frantically mad about a part of his family disobeying his last wishes.

'They couldn't wait for me to pop off,' he screeched. 'Then they dived in and helped themselves to my stuff.' Mrs Donald accepted the link, for he clearly told me: 'There was £400 that went to three and it should have gone to four.' Little wonder he was annoyed — someone had been robbed of their just monies. He also mentioned £200 and kept asking: 'What have they done with it? Where has it gone?' Mrs Donald said the family had sold his car for the meagre sum mentioned and there was annoyance because no one knew where the profits went.

Mention of 'the Cwm' and 'the organ-grinder and the blacksmith who lived next door' brought recognition, and to finish off his message her step-father wheeled himself to my side in a wheelchair. He had his right foot raised and heavily bandaged. 'That was the beginning of the end for me,' he said. There had been gangrene in the foot, which spread its poison through his body.

Another embarrassing incident involving a nasty communicator occurred when I was giving private appointments in a magnificent English Tudor mansion. I chuckle to think of it, even today. There I sat, on the blue silk couch, gazing around me thinking: 'I bet this carpet's worth more than my entire house.'

In sailed an elderly rich widow. I immediately sensed she'd lost her husband. Her thin mouth was set firm at 'twenty-past eight'. Yet, despite her stately elegance, she seemed very dour. She lowered herself down graciously, diamonds glinting, into the big Tudor armchair.

'Good morning,' I smiled. But silence was the icy reply, and her mouth never flinched. I was just about to launch into the messages when suddenly a small, old gentleman appeared on the antique sofa between us. How harassed he looked, and thoroughly hen-pecked. But there he sat, nonchalantly reading a newspaper, not at all bothered by my sitter's presence. I instantly knew that this was her husband. He peeped over his paper pathetically and said: 'She totally dominated me! Dying's the *best* thing that ever happened to me, my lad. I wouldn't go back to the old battleaxe for all the tea in China!'

Well, you could have knocked me off my chair with a feather! I was speechless.

'Listen,' he said, 'she's come in here today for you to tell her how wonderful she was, nursing me night and day. She wants a big pat on the back, my boy. But I'll tell you this — *I'm glad I'm dead*!'

How could I relay that? The old lady peered at me through her gold-rimmed spectacles, desperately awaiting some wonderful news from her husband; but would she really want to hear it?

Eventually I plucked up courage, stuttered a little and delivered what I still think is a masterful piece of tact. 'You've lost your husband, my dear,' I relayed, as her eyes lit up. 'And I must tell you that he's here with us today, sitting on that sofa.' She glowered across at the nothingness, probably relishing the prospect of ticking him off. 'And,' I continued, 'he wants me to tell you he's *very happy* where he is!'

Her stern face positively beamed with self-satisfaction. And the fixed mouth that came in set at 'twenty-past eight' left having risen to 'ten-to-two'!

I then sent her husband a sly thought: 'If you want to insult her, sir,' I said, 'you'll have to wait until she joins you, and do it yourself.'

'No, fear, lad,' he quickly replied. 'I'll be the other end of Eternity when *she* comes over!' And he chuckled away to himself for all he was worth.

When linking with the Other Side, some mediums find full names difficult to obtain; but these have featured in my work from the earliest days. Of course, I can't always be sensitive enough to receive them consistently, but on most occasions I'm fortunate to register them.

While giving a sitting to a Mrs Harris, I relayed that 'George' was present. She said she had known two of that name. I sent out a mental request, 'Which one do we have?', and back came the answer of 'Saunders.'

'Oh,' she exclaimed, with a twinkle in her eye, 'that's the

Stephen O'Brien, aged 8: 'I was slipping in and out of consciousness — I thought I was going to die and recited the Lord's Prayer over in my mind as they rushed me through the hospital doors.'

Stephen, his mother, Beatrice, and brother John: 'She was everything to us; someone very special. And I loved her with all my heart.'

'At 16, I wanted to enjoy living. I wanted to run free and feel the Great Pulse of Life in my veins.'

'I am your Guardian Spirit. My name is White Owl. Many on earth have lost their way and stumble through the Darkness of Ignorance; together we can bring them the Light of Knowledge. But I cannot do this alone — I need your help . . .'

World-famous psychic artist Coral Polge draws the spirit communicator, and Stephen provides the evidence.

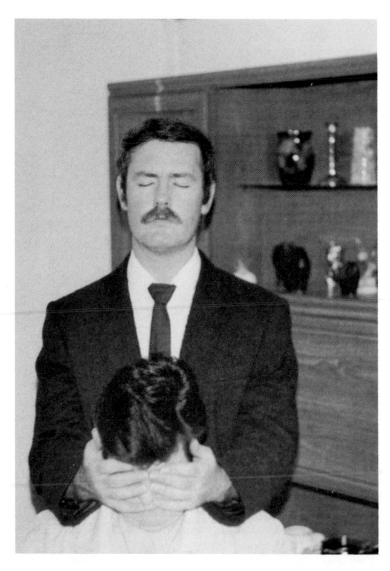

Delivering spiritual healing to a migraine sufferer.

Antony Hooper, 17, killed by the midnight train, returns to his mother via Stephen's mediumship.

Falklands hero, Ian Dale, 19, killed on the Sir Galahad when it exploded, gives his family evidence of his survival through Stephen's gifts.

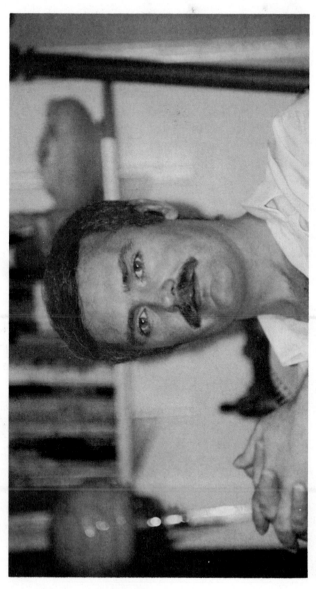

'I am a voice crying out a message of Hope from a World of Light. I've been called by the Spirit to serve, and I know, therefore, that my pathway will not be easy. But I pray God will give me the strength to complete what I was born to do.'

George I particularly liked when my maiden name was
Saunders!' I thought he was quite clever to have given it like
that.

Another woman would definitely *not* accept her grandmother
when I brought her. 'Come on,' I said, 'You'll have to give
something else. Be more specific.'

Well, she was! She brought up her whalebone corset, saying,
'Tell her I used to hang it behind the bedroom door and roll up
fivers and hide them down the whalebones.'

'That's her!' exclaimed the recipient. 'If you'd brought my
Grannie back any other way I couldn't have taken her.'

Other recipients look very confused when they're getting
their messages. One lady seemed awfully perturbed after I'd
taken great pains to describe a gentleman to her. In desperation
I finally asked, 'Well, does that sound like someone you know?'

'Oh, yes,' she said. 'It sounds like my grandad, but it can't be
— he's been dead *years*!' As if that made some difference!

Some sitters have cried with joy. Such as the lady who
received 'Bert' from the spirit-world. 'He's telling me to let you
know he's all in one piece now.' Her tears were instantaneous.

'Bert was my son,' she explained. 'He died tragically while
under a jacked-up car. Another car hit his and he was decapi-
tated.' She'd waited years for news of him. Little wonder she
cried when his contact came. 'Thank you so much. You'll never
know what that means to me,' she said.

I soon learned that the spirit-people could build a mental
impression in a medium's mind that could appear so real that
you might think you could reach out and touch it.

While once relaying information to a tearful lady from her
spirit father, I noticed she had a gold tooth right in the front of
her mouth. 'You don't see many of those these days,' I recall
thinking to myself.

At the end of the meeting, this lady came forward to thank me
for the link. But something was missing . . . 'Where's your
gold tooth gone?' I asked.

'I've never had one,' she said looking confused. Then she

suddenly screamed out with delight. She frantically opened her handbag and took out something wrapped in tissue-paper.

'My father's gold tooth!' she proudly announced. 'He was giving you the message when you saw it!'

I think my spirit-controls, the people working with me in a public demonstration, must have created the thought-form and superimposed it over the pictures in my mind. Aren't they clever?

Another time, Mrs Cole was so thrilled to hear from her husband in spirit that she almost left her seat when he said: 'Your tooth-filling's worked loose.'

'Oh! I've been three hours at the hospital today. No one else knew anything about it! How you could possibly have known!?'

'But I didn't know,' I said. 'Your husband told me.'

The spirit-people lost no time in making their presence felt — and they took every opportunity to do so. Once, while travelling back from a meeting, I suggested calling at my home for tea.

Dad never encouraged many visitors, and he wasn't in — so we piled out of the car and into the house. The lads quickly made themselves at home. Alan took the settee, kicked off his shoes and put his feet up, languishing with hands behind his head. John and I took a chair each. We chatted for a few minutes, when I began to feel uneasy. I was wondering what Dad's reaction would be if he found us by the blazing fire, supping tea. But before those thoughts had registered properly, a sudden psychic wind manifested through the room. It rapidly shook the closed door in its frame, sounding like violent thunder crashes, loud and alarming. The wind rushed through the door and towards me at amazing velocity and shot straight out through the window over my right shoulder. I was numbed. My mouth dropped open in disbelief as I quickly caught sight of two blurs whizzing past me — they were John and Alan. They bombed up the steps and into the car, leaving me to collect Alan's shoes and gingerly vacate the room saying 'Sorry' to the air as I left.

I discovered afterwards that my father had returned home

earlier than planned that night, not long after our undignified exit. Although it was a frightening warning it did seem to make sense of all those biblical quotes about the 'Wind of Heaven', and it certainly got the desired effect!

By now, some people were positive there was something decidedly 'odd' about me. Some, I'm sure, felt I was well on the way to madness. But nothing could have been further from the truth. These revelations were helping me to understand the deeper implications of life and living, instead of just skirting over the surface of existence as many seemed happy to do. Old friends 'walked by on the other side' and some positively veered away into stores to avoid speaking with me.

My neighbour, Florrie, had a cousin called Nancy. She was a lay-preacher and a very prim and proper lady. She was 70 years old and quite well respected in her orthodox church. But when she heard of my involvement with mediumship, she immediately branded me 'a devil's disciple' and ignored me at a bus-stop. Yet sadly, she had never seen a medium work or made an investigation into the paranormal.

I soon learned that the Other Side was not one bit concerned with labels or religions or lip-service codes of conduct. They were concerned with *people*. Souls, not labels. Before I helped someone I followed their example. I didn't ever ask what religious faiths they held. These are not the most important facets of our lives. We are people, struggling to find knowledge, seeking happiness or a little understanding. Seekers are curious to know about their loved-ones; whether they have survived. They want to know if they will see them again. They want communication with their dear people in spirit. I believe we are all children of the Great Spirit, and that's what I was being taught in those formative years. The spirit-people would often say we are all small sparks of the Great Spirit's Life-Force. This divine spark we each possess motivates us, gives us a conscious awareness and links us to the Creative Mind forever. We can never be separated from our Creator — the link remains eternally unbroken. Therefore we are all sons and daughters of that Living Mind, and if that is so then we are all brothers and sisters.

The spirit-people were teaching me that at all times I should strive to keep an open mind — and never close it. They asked that I should keep it open to new horizons of thought, new ideas and beliefs. And always they taught me to question everything I was told, no matter who said it. Even their own teachings were to be questioned, reasoned out, and accepted or rejected accordingly. Never once did they condone blind faith in anything. Never once did they dominate or patronize me or anyone they may have spoken to through my instrumentality. I came to believe that these were the hallmarks of evolved souls. I was often reminded: 'If you believe in anything 100 per cent, then this is dangerous. It is unhealthy because the mind is then closed to any new possibilities.' That sounded like good common sense to me.

I was also told, 'Seek and you will find. Knock and the door will be opened unto you.' This is as true today as it ever was. And to this they would add: 'Turn away and you may miss unique opportunities for greater happiness, knowledge and enlightenment. The choice is yours.'

Although each returning spirit person brought a different personal message, the content was broadly the same in many cases. They were met by those who loved them and knew them in the earth life. Only a few of them slept on arrival in spirit, and all found themselves alive and still very real people, complete with all their attributes of mind and character they had developed here on earth. Time after time they returned to categorically state that Over There they could clearly see that the only things which mattered were

> how we lived our lives;
> how we had thought;
> how we had acted.

Personal religious beliefs carried little weight Over There. But never once did they decry anyone's religion, rather did they say: 'If it makes you a better person, then it is right for you. If it teaches you to love, then it is a good set of instructions.'

I was soon invited to a Christian discussion group as my teachings spread further afield. I was delighted to accept and was requested to say a few words on the case for survival. I also looked forward to finding out what made other people tick.

We arrived at a neat semi-detached house and were ushered in and greeted by three ladies from the priest's church. Everyone was cordial and kind and we were getting along fine, when suddenly my arm was grabbed and I found myself being led away by the priest into a side study. He sat me down and respectfully warned me that 'We don't want any messages in here tonight, it's only a discussion.' I assured him that I had perfectly understood this when the invitation was offered. We joined the others.

After an evening of stimulating debate and many questions, the ladies' faces positively lit up when I revealed that everyone survived, regardless of their beliefs or station in life. But the priest then instantly closed the session — minus his curate who had quietly crept away, it all being too much for him I suspect — and told the listeners that if they investigated mediumship or visited a psychic or medium in the future, they would not be welcome at his church again.

As he left to get the coats, the ladies jumped out of their seats and bombarded me with a million questions, wanting the dates of my next meetings.

Our minds are such wonderful instruments, I'm often surprised when people don't use them to think matters out for themselves instead of accepting another's opinions. After all, what is true for one man need not be true for another.

By now, I'd heard through some friends of a spiritual healing group every Wednesday afternoon, so I decided to join that too and see if I could be of any help in this specific field.

Feeling light-headed, I'd close my eyes and deliver trance-healing to the patients. And once again, the spirit-world proved themselves and their powers. My hands would feel great warmth flowing through them, or they'd become icy cold;

physical reactions to different energy rays brought through by the spirit doctors who had attached themselves to me to work at healing the sick. Sometimes I didn't feel anything, no physical reaction at all. But the power was still evident, still working.

One day Mrs McDermot attended for healing. The Other Side drew very close to me as I stood behind her chair. I felt impressed to concentrate my efforts around her ears and head, touching her left ear and saying: 'I don't know what they're doing just here, and I can't feel any power passing through me, but they're most certainly doing *something*.' Unknown to me, she was completely deaf in that ear.

The next week, I could hardly take off my coat when Mrs McDermot dashed through the door and made straight for me with her exciting news. She'd woken up the following morning after the healing session and heard the ticking of the clock — something she hadn't done for years! She rushed to her specialist, breathless. He examined her and was totally dumbfounded. She recalled him exclaiming: 'I can't believe it. It's a miracle! The bones that were out of alignment have clicked back into their proper places. It's impossible! But somehow it's happened, and you can hear!'

As you can imagine, I continued my healing work after this. The spirit-doctors led me to a Mr Earnest Davies. I took a friend along with me to visit him at home because he was suffering from Multiple Sclerosis and wheelchair-bound. For 20 years the disease had held him in its merciless grip. Occasionally he would feel as though the world was turning upside-down; his arms would shoot out as if he was falling over and his head would be thrown back violently. After one visit, these unpleasant symptoms ceased, and to my knowledge have never recurred since.

Each week patients attended their sessions, and as my mediumship unfolded I began to grow more and more sensitive. One day a man attended for healing. He looked extremely unwell, but we exchanged pleasantries and then I realized I recognized him. He'd received a contact from his wife at my public demonstration a few days earlier. It was plain to see he respected my integrity, for he thanked me for the message.

Too weak to sit comfortably, he was placed on a healing couch and the healers gathered around, forming a kind of psychic battery of power. If I live to be a hundred I shall never forget the look in that man's eyes as he lay there, gazing up into my face. Those tearful eyes knew the fear of death and yet they longed for the success of this treatment. I gently smiled back at him.

'Try your best to relax,' I said. 'Please close your eyes.' As he did, he knew I'd read the secret of his heart. He had cancer, in a very progressed state. I also knew, unbearably, that his time had come and that healing could only ease the pain and make the passing more dignified and peaceful. But those haunting eyes, so full of pleading for a longer life, will always remain emblazoned in my memory as a reminder of the great faith, hope, and trust people place in spiritual healers when all orthodox medicine has failed. He passed into spirit a short while afterwards.

One glorious sunny day a middle-aged woman attended. She was fretful and looked extremely worried. The poor lady had the weight of the world on her shoulders. 'Can you please help me?' she begged, as she pulled from a bag a small boy's tee-shirt. 'My grandson's only six and he isn't at all well. We're out of our minds with worry. I brought this for you to hold to see if you can help him.'

Further questioning revealed that the boy was waking every night, screaming out for help. He'd told his grandmother that people were chasing him and that they came into his bedroom even when he was awake. The child was desperately afraid and distraught, and so were his parents because no amount of coaxing or common-sense explanations could pacify him.

I clutched the tee-shirt, and immediately felt the child's fear. We established that his name was David.

'I'll ask my spirit friends to help him tonight,' I told the anxious grandmother. 'Don't worry about him any more.

When you go to bed, send out your thoughts to your mother and father in the spirit-world and ask them to meet David at the point of sleep each night and take him into the sleep-life without any further distress.'

The woman looked at me agog. I suppose she couldn't figure out how I knew her parents had passed over. However, I went on to inform her that my spirit friends were impressing me that her grandson was wandering around in the astral planes of thought — those worlds nearest our earth on the Other Side — without any proper supervision.

'Yes, he's such an active mischief-maker,' she confessed, 'it would be just like him to run off on his own.'

'If you do as I suggest,' I added, 'then David won't be troubled again.'

She was profusely grateful and we parted company on the understanding that she would return only if the prescription had failed and the young lad remained unsettled.

Weeks passed by and her absence proved that all was well. People seem to think that mediums have the monopoly on the spirit-world, when communication is open to all. Sending out thoughts to our loved-ones often produces success, and no intermediaries are needed for us to accomplish that.

The doctors and healers who helped me on the Other Side were obviously following up this advice and keeping an eye on little David. And they proved their worth by bringing about the good results they'd promised a worried family.

The spirit-doctors were also perfectly correct when they intervened to aid a black Labrador dog called Prince after he had been injured. His owners thought he might have been involved in some accident with a vehicle but no one was certain. When I looked at Prince, and before I even approached him to place my hands gently on his glossy coat, I could see some words appearing above his body. They were 'fractured spine'. They hovered there for a moment, about three inches in depth and created in gold light.

'I think he could have injured his back,' I said to the lady. 'He may have even fractured the spine,' then I advised they immediately get a vet to examine him. This they did, and the diagnosis was a fractured spine, as the spirit-people had already perceived with their special kind of vision. Sadly, Prince was put to sleep because he was suffering from internal injuries, causing great pain afterwards. But nevertheless the owners 'saw' him shortly after his transition, sitting in his favourite spot by the kitchen door!

Healing works on animals as well as people. Healing is that ever-present, wonderful cosmic power, and it respects no particular person or organization, but will work its beneficent will whenever it is channelled and used correctly.

By now, I was becoming quite well-known in South Wales as a platform demonstrator and speaker. White Owl, who now worked closely with me from the Other Side, delivered trance addresses and gave thought-provoking philosophical teachings at all my meetings. This was followed by a display of clairvoyance. News was spreading fast about my work. London heard of it, and *Psychic News* printed reports of my mediumship. In this way, evidence and help I'd given to others reached a wide readership of over 100,000 people in 70 countries.

PSYCHIC NEWS

Stephen O'Brien gave evidence to Mrs Irene Lewis.

Stephen said her grandfather, Thomas, was present. He remembered working night-shifts to feed the family. This was correct.

In what became a family reunion, Stephen stated that Mrs Lewis' great-grandfather, William-John, her mother, Mary-Ellen, sister, Lily, and three brothers, John, Bryn and Harry, were all present.

Bryn sent love to Lorraine. This is his grand-daughter.

The medium relayed details of family history which Mrs Lewis confirmed as being correct. He said Mrs Lewis' brother, John, was involved with Orthodox clergy. He was a Baptist Missionary.

Stephen added that Mary-Ellen had four sisters with her in

the spirit-world. He described Mary-Ellen's abdominal troubles caused by difficult childbirth.

The 74-year-old widow was startled when Mary-Ellen recalled a traumatic incident from her childhood.

When Mrs Lewis was nine she ran home breathless and frightened after being chased across the fields by a man. Even after 65 years the reminder of the event still disturbed her.

A neighbour, Mrs Simmons, passed on her thanks to Mrs Lewis for running errands for her when she could not leave the house many years before.

Finally, Mrs Lewis' husband, Bill, was named by the medium as being present.

He correctly related the communicator had suffered from a blockage of the bowel and passed with cancer of the stomach.

Through the medium, Mr Lewis told of his sense of shame in being a burden during his long illness. He was in no pain now.

After the spontaneous sitting Stephen left to demonstrate at a Spiritualist church, but not before Mrs Lewis had presented him with a small token of thanks: A tin of baked beans.

'I'm not a Spiritualist,' said Mrs Lewis, 'but it made me think. I found the experience very touching.'

'I now feel my loved ones are closer to me. My sense of loneliness has been wiped away.'

'Stephen is a very good person,' she said, 'whom I think lives what he believes.'

'It is marvellous that God is using him as a medium to show us there is a life after death.'

9
Séances

People from all walks of life, from all over the world, have sought my help; many coming as a last desperate hope, their lives shattered by tragedy, or their pathway so dark that they pleadingly requested some kind of light to show the way forward. Some of these people were so moved by their communications that they recorded them, and many of these sitters freely undertook the development of their own psychic powers as a direct result of being touched by the spirit. When their consultations with me are over, at the end of the day it is only the sitters themselves who can truly judge what the messages have meant to them. So, it's fitting to include a random selection of their accounts here, where they can relate the effects they experienced in their own words.

The first report concerns friendship and its undying nature:

Mr Adrian Davie, college lecturer

My friend died in an accident and his death devastated me. I felt it should never have happened because he was killed as a pedestrian when a car mounted the hard shoulder of the road and instantly ended his life. This was the first time death had touched me and I felt lost, hurt and depressed at the time.

Mr Stephen O'Brien gave my wife and me spontaneous clairvoyance. He said he could see 'a pair of leather motorbike gauntlets plus a red crash helmet suspended in the air' over my shoulder. This identified to me my friend, Alan, whom I worked with for six years. Alan had given me these two items as a gift about a year prior to his death. The medium brought him forward as being '21 years old' — the correct age at his death.

Further evidence was given when Mr O'Brien said that Alan was showing him 'a skull and crossbones motif, painted somewhere'. I couldn't recall this, but my wife reminded me that three days before this message I'd taken her to Sunderland Museum where there was a photographic exhibition, which included a photograph of my working place. And this same motif was painted on a cabin door in a photograph. Alan used to work in that place.

This made me realize that he still visited me at work as Mr O'Brien had relayed. To confirm this further Alan gave Mr O'Brien the name of 'Brian'. Brian is the person who has taken my friend's place as my workmate.

Next came a meaningful piece of information. The medium said 'He keeps saying "Broken back".' This was the nickname Alan had for me at work. When I was doing heavy work he used to say: 'You'll break your back doing that.' More remarkable still was that I saw Alan's death certificate and a broken back as well as other injuries was listed on it.

I was elated to receive this evidence. This was the first time my friend had ever made contact with me in the six years since his death. When this message came from him it was as though I had found his friendship again, as though he had never died. He had proved his identity to me without a shadow of a doubt. It could not have been any other person but him, and there is no way Mr O'Brien could have known any of these details Alan gave.

Alan's message to me was 'I only died', as though death was nothing at all. It has showed me that the 'dead' are not in a distant world but are close by, their lives intertwining with ours without us realizing it.

If there was more evidence like this, the sorrow of grieving people would be swept aside.

Another account clearly shows us that the spirit-people can travel all over our world, faster than the speed of light, and know what is happening long before news of it reaches us physically. Most times, this fact surprises sitters:

Mrs Marion Jones, shop manageress

Stephen O'Brien described to me a peasant grandmother figure whom he clairvoyantly saw sitting in the sun outside a wooden shack. She was cleaning corn-cobs. He told me she was thanking me for helping her grandson and she was giving him the word 'Cruz'. He was puzzled by this word and wondered if it was the name of a place in South America. But it was not that at all. Something he could not possibly have known was that the word 'Cruz' is the surname of a 10-year-old Mexican boy whose education I am sponsoring. The boy is called Serafin Aragon Cruz.

I was stunned to receive this news because the Cruz family live thousands of miles away from me — right round the other side of the world — and yet Serafin's grandmother in the next life not only knew of our association but also had taken the trouble to give her approval and thanks.

The spirit-people can also 'follow' our progress through life, and in many cases they are walking beside us, often unregistered. This next account proves that a lady who was on her way to her usual Methodist church, was most certainly followed:

Mr Will Ford, church president

Mr O'Brien's clairvoyance contained the highest level of evidence I'd heard for some years. He told my daughter she was linked with the medical profession. She is a tutor in St Mary's Teaching Hospital, London. He also said a doctor friend of hers had just received some good news. That week, her doctor-friend had been accepted as a consultant. Mentioning she was concerned over a lady's health was correct, as she was deeply concerned over the health of her mother. The medium then gave details of a lady in spirit who had given this information. Without question, it was my mother.

The medium spoke to my sister: 'What are you doing here?

You're in the wrong church! You were on your way to your own church, you changed your mind, you walked past your own church and came here instead.'

This was quite true. When my sister left home she had no intention of coming to our church whatsoever. The medium told her that her husband had died some years ago and that she hadn't yet got over the shock. This is true. My sister is under medical care for delayed shock. He then gave a lot of information which could only have been from her husband in the spirit-world.

The spirit people can often 'tune-in' to our thoughts, and once they have developed this ability, there are no secrets! They live in a world where thought is king, and even though we on earth can hide the truth by closing our mouths or speaking untruths — the mind cannot lie! Mrs Round's youngest daughter kept a secret from her mum, but her grandfather in the spirit world 'read' it, and predicted an event that subsequently occurred:

Mrs D. Round, nursing officer

One of the most surprising pieces of information Mr O'Brien relayed was from my deceased father concerning the youngest of my three daughters, whom he said would be the first to marry and that this would happen in the very near future. The statement seemed ridiculous, as my daughter was so young. I laughed at the thought. But my father laughed last, for he was correct in all he had said; my youngest *was* the first to be married.

This brought a realization that my father was aware of what was in the minds of the youngsters involved although, at the time, they believed it to be their secret.

Some messages seem quite trite and uninteresting when they are delivered publicly — but then the medium and the public have no true understanding of just exactly what a message means to a recipient, or the way in which it will affect them, or in many instances change their lives. Many sitters have found

their spirit-contacts touchingly encouraging, and have gained
new strength and hope from them:

Mrs Sandy Meakin, housewife

I went to see you at Doncaster. You called out for a Sandra and
said there was a family around me which was breaking my
heart. This I accepted. You brought me a 'rag-and-bone cart
and a gypsy man called Sam'. This, too, I accepted. You then
gave me Alice-Mary. This was my grandmother's name, and
you said she and Sam were taking care of me. Then you said
there was a gentleman with me who had passed quickly with a
heart attack, he was around 39 — 40 years old. He gave me red
roses from a wedding bouquet and you gave me September and
felt he was a husband. The names Wilf and Violet were also
relayed. These people were my husband and mother-in-law,
and the 11th September was his birthday.

This proof has been second to none and I thank you from the
bottom of my heart, for you not only gave me the strength to go
on but you also gave me a ladder of life to climb, and I am still
climbing it. I will remember this for the rest of my life.

As a visionary, I seldom get to see the sitters when they arrive
for their consultation; there is usually a receptionist or chaper-
one ushering them in, making them tea afterwards and gener-
ally placing them at ease. This next record, then, is of particular
interest to me.

Mr J. Rees-Jones, sculptor and Oxfam worker

I've acted as receptionist for some of Mr O'Brien's private
consultations and I've witnessed many different reactions from
folk. Often they get something quite unexpected. Like the
gentleman who emerged rather flushed after a good telling-off
from his father who was unhappy about his son's lifestyle,
showing us that even after death we still remain uniquely
human, keeping all our character traits.

Or the lady who emerged so astonished she was almost
speechless after receiving such accurate evidence, all she could

repeat was: 'I don't believe it. How could he know?'

There have been many tearful and emotional reunions too. Mothers have found their children after agonizing years of searching. Partners have been brought together again convinced by pet-names that no one else could have known. And some leaving unconvinced have been directed by their contacts to research certain facts that they had no knowledge of at the time. Then they came back to tell me they'd found them to be true!

When you've seen a mother weep with relief, finally knowing her 'lost' child is safe and alive, then you truly realize the full importance of mediums and their work.

The media seem to fail to understand that many who have received personal messages from Beyond, from the people they dearly love, do not want this made public knowledge — in just the same way as most family matters are private and confidential. Private consultations are exactly that — *private*. Many accounts are so touchingly personal I couldn't possibly allow them to be printed, and I know the sitters would agree with my witholding them. The following record of events is such a case. Mrs Williams' only daughter was murdered by brutal raiders on the shop where she worked, and her letter to me contains many comments about my work and personality, and her gratitude, which I feel are too moving to print. I therefore have released only part of her account.

At her sitting, Mrs Williams' daughter made a specific request to her mother. 'Please don't go to the Inquest,' she asked.

'I'm sorry,' returned Mrs Williams, 'but tell her I'll have to go. I couldn't sit at home while it's in progress.' And much later Mrs Williams did attend it. It was only then that the true horrific details of her daughter's death were publicly released and the reason for her request from beyond death made plain. The young mother had been bludgeoned to death and then assaulted. The murderers then doused her body with petrol but fled without setting it alight.

Mrs Elizabeth Williams, voluntary adult education worker

I was holidaying in Italy when my only daughter was brutally murdered during a robbery. We were, as a family, stunned and almost completely broken. When I felt I was ready I had a sitting with Stephen O'Brien. And here I must make it quite clear that he knew nothing of my life before the events mentioned.

He did, however, bring my father, my husband and my daughter through to me with details he could not have possibly known. This was a great comfort to us all, and during the following months, it was a tower of strength to me. And I can never thank Mr O'Brien enough.

At the time of writing, I received a spirit-message through a northern medium, who mentioned the name Emrys Williams to me, who was saying: 'Thank you for helping my family.' This man is Mrs Elizabeth Williams' husband in the spirit-world, and he obviously knew of her account being included in this volume, for he mentioned 'the writings' during his link. I immediately contacted Mrs Williams to let her know of his connection with me, and she commented: 'That's so typical of Emrys — he wouldn't want to be left out!'

10

Spirit Children

Spirit-children often visit me and it's always a great joy to see them. They bring feelings of light and energy, a quick, fine vibration of youthful enthusiasm. Their eyes are bright and open wide, and yet behind them there seems to be an inner-knowing that very few earth children possess.

But they do seem to choose the oddest times to call. Once, I'd just whipped into the bath to freshen up when I heard a woman's voice speak to me from mid-air.

'Stephen, I'm bringing some children to see you.'

'But I'm having a bath!' I said in disbelief, grabbing the nearest sponge. But the voice continued.

'They need education. They haven't lived on earth. They're still-born babies and miscarriages who have reached childhood on our side. This could be one of their lessons, if you are willing.'

'Okay,' I said, modestly gathering the suds together. The voice went on to ask me if I would tell them what sort of daily activities we get up to on earth. I'd always thought of myself as a teacher and I love children very much, which is why they were brought to me; plus the fact that mediums shed more psychic light about them and it's easier for spirit-visitors to view our atmosphere from their world if a sensitive is present.

There wasn't a great deal of water in the bath-tub, but it didn't stop these beautiful children of all nationalities trying their hardest to splash it around. They were tittering and giggling at 'the pink man sitting in the bath'. They whispered confidentially amongst each other, just as children do, and they asked me so many questions. One second they were all visible, and the next my vision faded — but although my psychic sight tuned in and out of their presence, they were still there, chattering away and having a marvellous time. It must have been like a trip to the zoo for them!

'What does water feel like?', they asked; 'Does it hurt you?' 'What's that fluffy stuff you're getting on your skin?' I explained all about soap. In fact, after receiving a telepathic request from their teacher, I went into explanations about why we on earth needed to wash our skins. And their eyes almost popped out of their heads when I ended up with: 'And I have a bath every day.' I don't think they could believe that one!

One coloured girl said: 'Our water doesn't make us wet. It rolls off our skins.' And this isn't difficult to accept if their water behaves in a similar fashion to, say, mercury.

So there I was, an hour to go before a public meeting, sitting in a few inches of bathwater, holding a conversation with 'dead' children. Yet how natural and commonplace it all seemed.

At the end of our class, as they all left I heard the children giggle and the teacher said to me: 'A picture is worth a thousand words.' I suppose that's very true when you think about it.

Another amusing appearance of a spirit-child occurred when I was baby-sitting for my brother. He was working nightshift, and my sister-in-law was sleeping at the hospital with my nephew, Johnathan, who was due to undergo an eye operation. I was asked to look after my niece, Claire, and they gave me Johnathan's bed.

Try as I might, I couldn't go to sleep. All the hairs on my legs were standing on end. There were so many electric presences near the room and I became very conscious that these were spirit-children gathering around the bed, no doubt having a good look at the great hulk sleeping there, when they expected to see my five-year-old nephew. Suddenly, I felt the hairs on my right leg being tweaked. I opened my eyes and there standing at the foot of the bed was a young lad of about seven years, sporting blonde curls and a wicked smile, a good match for Johnathan. He just couldn't understand who I was or what I was doing there.

'Well, where *is* he then?' he demanded, frowning hard. I immediately knew I shouldn't frighten him with Johnathan's operation details, so I whispered out: 'He's on holiday for a few days. He'll be back on Monday.' Of course, it never dawned on me at the time that the spirit-people don't follow our calendar and dates. However, this little chap turned his head and indignantly called out over his shoulder to an invisible person: 'Oh, he's gone away!'

As I held back a smile, a spirit-nurse appeared behind him. 'Come along, Daniel,' she scolded, 'I told you he wasn't here, didn't I?' And she clasped his hand tightly and led him out through the bedroom wall. The psychic atmosphere in the room calmed down, and after that I slept soundly. But I couldn't help grinning when I imagined young Daniel coming to collect Johnathan for his nightly visit to the spirit-world and discovering me instead! And if you think about it, it's perfectly natural that he should pull the hairs on my leg. After all, Johnathan didn't have any.

But not all my spirit-children have returned with happy, radiant faces. At one meeting in Hitchin, Hertfordshire, a singing trio were just rendering their final song before I gave my clairvoyance, when a pathetic-looking boy appeared to my psychic vision, just at the side of my chair. 'I'm Tommy,' he said, as I greeted him mentally, asking him why he had come. He then coughed up some black matter, which I thought was probably blood, and said: 'I'm three. I had TB.'

This boy was accepted by one of the singers in the group when a link with 'Streatham Green' was mentioned. And when Tommy said he wanted 'John to know I love him and miss him very much', the singer told the audience this was his small brother. Everyone smiled with him and I when he comically said: 'Mum's washed out my teddy-bear and she's pegged him on the line'! He didn't seem too happy about that. This information was to be checked, and if it was correct, how marvellous to know that a little lad like Tommy was aware of his teddy-bear's bath. He asked the singer, 'Please get Mum to come to a meedjum, 'cos I want to talk to her.'

I can't describe the wonderful feeling I have when this kind of link is made and new hope is put into a grieving person's life. Anyone who has lost a child will know how tremendously touching this sort of communication can be to witness. I feel a great attunement and empathy with parents who have lost little ones, because when I have been able to link them all together, I have become — even for a short while — a part of the family.

I've learned that still-born babies or children who aren't carried for their full term of pregnancy all survive death and grow up on the Other Side. There they're loved and cared for by people who dedicate their lives to rearing them, just as good parents do here.

To back these claims, I once received a disturbing message, and didn't quite know how to relay it. Seated opposite me was a young, carefree girl, wearing cut-off jeans. Her hair was adorned with coloured rags and beads. It was a deep sandy colour, but it was unkempt and in need of grooming. She had intellectual blue eyes and compassion shone from her. When I tuned in to the spirit-world, however, I lost sight of her because my attention was drawn to a golden ball of light appearing on her lap. It was shot through with electric blue sparks, like a thousand stars. And in the centre of this pulsating, protective orb was a human foetus — all curled up and perfectly formed, just as it would be in its mother's womb. Then this vision faded into the young woman's body, and vanished. In that instant, a young girl of about four years faded into sight, kneeling in front of this woman, with her head resting on her hands placed across the woman's knees. The child looked at me. She had the same piercing eyes as the lady, and the same sandy-coloured hair.

'She's my Mummy,' she said. A spirit helper informed me

the girl had been aborted four years ago, and would I tell the woman she had a daughter in the spirit-world, and one day they'll be together again. But how could I give this out in public? I couldn't. I had to find a clever way of putting it across, to save any embarrassment and yet get the message home. Eventually I said to the woman: 'I think you know a lady who lost a child before it was born.'

'Yes,' she replied weakly, her eyes searching the floor.

'Well,' I continued, 'the girl is now four years old, and please would you tell her mother that she's alive in the spirit-world and that one day they'll meet up? That would make the little girl very happy.' The surprised woman thanked me, and I knew that in delivering it that way, I'd done my job and wrapped up the message so that no one else would understand it except the recipient.

Then there was the time I was called in to investigate and help out with a haunting. The parents of little Stephen, a five-year-old, had been woken up in the night by singing coming from his bedroom. They knew it wasn't *his* voice they could hear, so they called me in to solve the riddle.

We all mounted the stairs and I was led into little Stephen's room. The moment I moved within the door, I felt uneasy; glancing at the window, which overlooked a steep drop to a roof and then down to a garden, I could see a spirit-girl standing. She was in need of a wash. But nevertheless there she was, singing away to me to her heart's content. I couldn't make out her childish song, but I could clearly see her stretching out her hand and crooking her little finger and beckoning me to go to the window. I obeyed, and in that instant, once I'd approached her spirit-form, it was as though a flash of lightning had struck my senses. I saw the whole pitiful tale before me. I turned to Stephen's parents:

'This room was once a kitchen,' I stated.

'Oh, yes — years ago it was,' said the mother. 'The estate agent told us that when we bought the house recently.'

'Well, I've seen a small girl just there.' And I gave a

description of her singing, adding: 'She was at the open kitchen window, she climbed onto the ledge and slipped. She fell to her death onto the roof and into the garden below.'

There was stunned pause. The mother looked rather worried.

'Your son likes to climb out onto ledges, doesn't he?' I asked.

'Yes,' she said pathetically. Then I told the parents to stop fretting and worrying because my spirit-people would now take the child and make sure that she was safe, and that no recurrence of these events would happen. That didn't satisfy them though. They didn't like the idea of being in a haunted home. Then, I heard my spirit-friends giving me another message.

'You needn't worry, you'll soon be moving from here anyway.'

'But we've only just bought it!' protested the mother, adding it was their family home. Even though the place was 'haunted' she had no intention of moving out.

'But your spirit-people will arrange it for you,' I said confidently. And of course, they did. They moved away shortly afterwards as predicted. I don't know what became of the little spirit-girl in the pink dress, but the young lad has now grown and I'm told he was no longer lured out onto ledges by his mischievous spirit-visitor.

The saddest case of a spirit-child returning was that of a young girl of seven who had been kidnapped, sexually assaulted, and murdered. To protect her parents, I shall call the girl Sarah. The newspapers were emblazoned with her tragic death and its details, and a major police-hunt was underway to seek the killer. She was returning home from school across woodland when her life was so cruelly taken.

I was so upset to read the sordid story that I cried, and in absolute despair for this child I found myself uttering: 'Dear God, someone please comfort her, wherever she is. Help her, anyone who can hear me.' Thoughts of her desperate mother flooded my mind and only served to increase the grief I shared with this distant family whom I'd never met. I didn't then realize it, but my sympathetic thoughts had linked me with their cry for help. And through this link, the spirit-world took action.

Thoughts are living things, and White Owl is rather good at registering them. As proof of this, the following day, during my silent meditation time, I felt a strange presence about me; someone I didn't know was drawing close and activating my psychic senses. I heard a child's voice crying, pitifully sobbing. That little girl was Sarah, the murdered child. White Owl had sought her out and brought her near to me.

'Tell my Mummy I'm alive,' she sobbed. 'She's crying, and she can't see me. Please tell my Mummy I'm alive.'

Poor Sarah was distraught. White Owl explained she had been to see her family on earth, but not one of them had then been able to register her presence sufficiently enough for good communication to take place.

Instinctively I knew what to do. No time should be wasted. I was inspired to write to her family with the message of their daughter's survival, but first I answered Sarah's tears: 'I will do everything I can,' I said. 'Don't worry, Sarah; I'll get in touch with your Mummy, and then she'll know you're alive and well.' I then gently instructed her to follow White Owl who would take her to her relatives in the Beyond. She seemed to calm at this, and then her presence faded from my consciousness. I was firmly back in my sitting-room. Grabbing the nearest pen, I sent a card to Sarah's people — the newspaper had the address in it, or at least a part of the address. Comforting myself that my mail would reach its destination on a wing and a prayer — and a little help from White Owl — I posted it off immediately.

Days passed by and I heard nothing from Sarah's mother. Did she receive my card? Had it been mislaid? What if Sarah contacted me again — what could I tell her? Many thoughts clouded my mind. Perhaps the mother had read my words telling her that Sarah was 'alive in another world, and grieves because you are crying so bitterly over your loss. But please be happy in the knowledge that Sarah lives on, and is close to you', and maybe she thought the letter had come from someone unbalanced. I could only sit and wait and rest easy knowing my job was done.

A fortnight later, a reply arrived. It was a thank-you card, expressing gratitude for the message and assuring me that Sarah's mother had indeed felt that her daughter was often with her. The relief expressed in those words was clear to see, and I thanked White Owl.

I never did see Sarah again. She didn't return to thank me herself, although I was told she passed her gratitude on. But the greatest satisfaction comes from quietly knowing I've tried to help in small ways.

When Carla's mother came to see me, she was desperate for help. Carla was 10 when she died. She'd complained of a headache to her Mum, who advised her to lie down for a while and rest. But when her mother called her for tea, there was no reply.

Frantically, she clambered up the stairs — something within her telling her something was very wrong. And her feelings were sadly correct. Carla had passed away. The coroner's verdict was a massive brain haemorrhage. You can imagine how Carla's mother felt. One moment her happy daughter had been skipping out in the park and within an hour she had gone from her life forever. She was so utterly distraught. Just as soon as she could, she visited her local clergyman. But unfortunately he was unable to offer any help. In fact, quite the reverse. He aggravated Carla's mother by telling her that because Carla had not been confirmed into his faith or officially accepted by his Church, that she would now be burning in the 'fires of hell'.

Utterly desperate when she sought my help, I readily agreed to a sitting. Somewhere in a book, not unknown to that clergyman, it is written: 'And a little Child shall lead them.' And this was most certainly so in this case.

I'd only just started the communications when Carla appeared to my vision, seated on the settee, right beside her mother. She had her arm about her shoulders and she carried her 'special' doll, which — when I described it in detail — proved Carla's survival.

'I'm alright,' she told her mother. 'My head was hurting me and when I went to lie down, I heard a sound like an explosion and then Grandad met me.' She named him correctly, and then passed on much comforting evidence to her relieved mother. When the lady left, she was a totally transformed being. The stooped, grieving woman who entered an hour before was now once again a radiant, happy mother. She had found her child. She was alive, not dead. She was living in a land not far removed from here, but nearer than hands and feet. Once more, the link of love through mediumship had mended a broken life. And when all the excitement dies away, and the sun rises on each new day, what remains is the fact that we are immortal beings, and that our broken lives are once more made whole by the truth.

Nothing could be more poignant than the recent loss of human life in Britain's conflict over the Falkland Islands, those distant rocks so far from our shores. Talk of patriotism and defending the Realm probably means so very little to the parents of the young men killed in those battles. However, hope is not yet gone.

Young Ian Dale, 19, was a Welsh Guardsman in the newly-formed Mortar Platoon. He was down below decks of the Sir Galahad when an Argentinian bomb from a plane shot down a hatch and ignited the ammunition pile he and his platoon were guarding.

This young lad and his friend both communicated to me one night. The contact went to a lady at the back of the hall.

'You know this boy's mother,' I said. And with that a woman at the front called out, 'Here I am.' And sure enough it was indeed her. She was sitting with Ian's father. The young Guardsman spoke to his 'Mam and Dad', assuring them he was well on the Other Side. His best friend also communicated his survival. And then the boy told his mother about a special tie he had given to someone.

'No,' she said holding up an object clasped tightly in her hands. 'He means this button off his cap.'

What could I say? Ian was mentioning a tie, not a button. So I gently repeated the message, apologizing if I'd misheard it, but nevertheless holding on firmly to my link. I suddenly was aware that she'd come into the meeting hoping for some contact with him, at her wit's end and in need of comfort. Again Ian said to me: 'It's a special tie I gave away, Mum.' And we had to leave it at that. Despite a quiet chat with Mrs Shirley Dale later, I was disappointed not to have been more helpful. But it's strange how things work out, because about six months later a lady brought me some tea after a public meeting.

'You don't remember me, do you?' she said. I confessed she was right. And she identified herself as Ian's mother, expressing her profuse thanks. 'I researched the evidence about that tie,' she told me, 'and he'd given it to his brother, Phillip, the day he packed for the Falklands trip. I was amazed because we knew nothing about it.' After this, she joined her local Spiritualist Church and now makes tea and helps out in whatever way she can, trying to repay the great debt of help she and her grieving family received from the movement's mediums. 'I owe my sanity to Spiritualism,' she said.

Then there was the case of young Robert. He was only 16. He had been out on his motorbike riding casually along the roads when a police car, moving rather fast, came into collision with him — he died instantly. His family were devastated; the Thomases could not believe it had happened. For a long time afterwards, they tried to prove that the fault lay with the police, and not their son. And so their search began to find him again.

About three years after his death, they attended a large public meeting of mine, and Robert made a surprising contact. His mother takes up the story in her own words:

I attended a demonstration of mediumship by Mr Stephen

O'Brien and received a message from my son, who had been deceased for three years. The message contained irrefutable evidence that it was from Robert, and it was accurate. It mentioned how his body was mutilated, his ambitions about getting a bigger bike, and also that his sister still cries for him. Robert even spoke of 'a secret girlfriend'. We only found out about her three weeks before the message. She wrote to us to find out how he was getting along now. A lot more evidence was given too, details about his leather jacket with the studs on the back and he told the medium to 'give Dad a kiss from me'.

My son was killed in a collison with a police car while riding his 30 mph limited speed bike on a straight piece of road. What the police said enabled the blame to be thrown onto my dead son, who couldn't speak for himself.

We have always had strong suspicions that this was not the case. This opinion was held by our solicitor also, but due to how the statements of witnesses were obtained, we couldn't prove it.

The point Robert wanted to get across to us most strongly was to say, 'Please, please tell my Mum *it wasn't my fault.*' I cannot express the sense of relief this evoked in us. It was a message we had waited three years for. You can imagine my feelings.

I must say that I feel great respect and admiration for Mr Stephen O'Brien and the work that he does, and I am unable to convey the peace of mind he brings to those who are grieving with such messages as this from the spirit-world.

Psychic News, London, carried a report on the evidence, as did three of Mr and Mrs Thomas's local papers. As a result of this the church for whom the meeting was held noted an increase in interest and many new people attended their meetings. So from the happiness of two people, the good news spread and touched others.

There is nothing more touching than when the young die. And nothing more beautiful than when they return. Over the years, many have done so through mediumship, and I have felt greatly privileged to have helped them reach their families. There was young Phillip who locked himself in a discarded refrigerator and was found days later; Trudy and her two brothers who burned to death in a house blaze and left their mother and father desolate and alone, and pitifully wondering 'Why?'; John, who drank from a bottle of household bleach, thinking it was lemonade — they rushed him to the hospital, but it was too late; and scores of others, all returning with the same message: 'I'm alive, don't cry for me.' But none made a bigger impact upon me than the case of Antony Hooper. His was a tragic passing, and the one I've recorded in the greatest detail for this book.

Antony was just 17 when he was tragically killed by the midnight sleeper-train to Paddington. A British Transport Police spokesman told the court that foul play was ruled out and that Antony's leather jacket, gold watch and a £5 note had been discovered alongside the railway track. Coroner Mr Francis Wilson admitted his death could have been suicide, but instead an open verdict was recorded. Consultant Pathologist Dr Owen Williams said Antony's death was due to multiple injuries sustained by contact with a moving train.

His entire family were deeply shocked by the news of his death and couldn't come to terms with his passing at all. His mother had said goodbye to him at four o'clock and never saw him alive again. For her, each day had no meaning now. On buses, watching other people smiling and laughing, she just couldn't understand why life continued so normally. She didn't recognize it then, but she was suffering from acute shock.

As a last desperate hope, she decided to seek out a medium. If her son was alive 'somewhere', she wanted to know about it. She wanted to hear from him, find out how he was, who was taking care of him — if he existed after death?

Taking her courage in both hands, she attended several Spiritualist churches for seven months, always keeping her identity secret, never speaking to anyone about her quest, to make any word from him all the more evidential — if it came. But sadly, no contact was made.

Psychic News takes up the story:

A mother spent seven months visiting Spiritualist churches in search for contact with her teenage son who passed tragically. She finally received her reward, a communication through Stephen O'Brien.

'I was so overjoyed. I just couldn't take it all in,' she told *Psychic News*. 'At last I had found my son.'

Mrs Maureen Hooper had seen many mediums demonstrating.

'Although I believed that mediums were able to make contact with people who had passed over, upon searching I have found this is not the case in many instances,' she said. 'Even on a purely psychic level, dozens of mediums have failed to recognize my grief and the fact that I have lost a son.'

As Mrs Hooper's search progressed she prayed for a message from her son, Antony. Yet each time she was given a message, there was no mention of him.

'Nevertheless I kept going,' she told *Psychic News*, 'living in the hope that he would reach me and prove his survival.'

'My hopes were shattered, and disillusionment set in. I wondered many times where I, and other grieving parents like me could go to be given comfort via sure proof of survival.

'All I was mostly given were "nuns", "sisters of mercy", "bouquets of roses" and "colourful rainbows". Where was my son among this? Was this the highest standard mediums could attain? Or was I expecting too much?'

Mrs Hooper had almost given up hope when she found an advertisement in her local newspaper for a demonstration of mediumship. Deciding to attend, she was surprised at the high quality of detailed evidence, which included full names, place names and accurate dates.

'At last I received a great deal of hope. I continued my search by following the mediumship of Stephen O'Brien, and at his third meeting, Mr O'Brien brought my son back to me with amazingly evidential details.

'I was given his name, his father's name, and the circumstances leading up to his tragic passing. This medium even told me who was looking after him in the spirit-world, Mary Jane, a great aunt.

'At the time of the communication, Mr O'Brien even seemed

to take on my son's personality; there was a great deal of comforting evidence relayed.

'Isn't it a shame that the majority of mediums do not concentrate on bringing back our loved-ones and proving their survival without doubt? While I appreciate that some try to do this, why can't they all?'

I first saw Mrs Hooper seated in a crowd and as she left I rushed to clasp her hand, recognizing her state of grief, and said: 'I don't know who you've lost, but if you hold on a while longer, I'm told they're trying to get through.'

Her big eyes widened, and she could barely say 'thank you' as she left. But a few weeks later, Antony's link arrived. It contained many factual details not printed above, small evidential remarks which conveyed his personality and style.

Prior to his passing, Antony had stolen a car and taken a joyride with three other boys. The car had crashed and was a writeoff. Antony made his way across fields to reach his father's Auto Garage, and those were his last moments on earth — the railway tracks stood in his path.

When communicating, he mentioned these events, talked of personal family matters, and also commented on 'new central heating installed', adding, 'It's about time too!' Mrs Hooper said this was a typical remark, especially as the heating had been planned for years and never materialized while he was on earth.

It was too late to tell anyone that night when Mrs Hooper got home, but as soon as she could, absolutely everyone heard about her son's first words from beyond death. When she told his father on the telephone, he had to hang up and within 10 minutes he'd left work and was sitting in her front room, eagerly listening to the story. Antony's elder brother Gary held on to his mother and cried, just sobbing with relief and once again touched by the loss. And Phillip, his younger brother, listened intently, numbed by the news.

After his initial contact, Mrs Hooper was so overwhelmed and grateful that we got talking and eventually I became friends with her and her family. This meant that we had not heard the last from Antony Hooper. He had now found his medium and he was determined to make use of him.

He notified his family that he was studying on what he called 'a contact course' in the Beyond, to learn how to transmit his messages correctly. And he proved a good student too, for we heard from him again very soon.

One evening, when I was speaking with the family, I heard Antony's distinctive voice calling to me. Taking up paper and pen, I wrote down his statements exactly as he said them, and they turned out not only to be evidential but to display an intelligent carefully worked out set of comments, many of them having to be checked afterwards in a bid to rule out telepathy by his medium. And he was successful. I can't read facts from someone's mind if the information isn't there. He knew this would be more convincing to his Mum. Here is what Antony transmitted, word for word:

ANTONY	RESEARCH
My jeans were fought over by my two brothers after I passed. But it didn't matter to me who had them.	Correct. Checked out, and Gary and Phillip had fought over his black canvas jeans. This was the first Mrs Hooper had heard of this.
My pair of yellow briefs. There was a small hole in them and they were thrown out.	Correct. He tore them in an embarrassing accident.
I wanted a racing pigeon, but didn't manage to get one.	Checked. Accurate. His best friend kept racing pigeons and he would have liked one.
My thick belt, with the large buckle and studs on it. I don't know where that went. Did they burn it with me? I want to know.	His brother Gary had secretly kept it as a memento.

ANTONY	RESEARCH
Who's been thinking of my birth certificate? I've received the thoughts, but don't know who it is.	Phillip, the youngest, had been searching for it that morning, unknown to Mrs Hooper.
There is one single daisy growing by my stone on the cemetery floor.	EXPEDITION!

This final remark bundled us into a car with some torches, and we were off to the cemetery. It was two o'clock in the morning and bitingly cold with no moon. We crept through the church gates into the chill graveyard and found Antony's stone. And there, right beside it, was *one solitary daisy*. There were no others — just this one, exactly where he'd said it was.

We were dumbfounded. No flowers were out at that time, yet this single daisy had freshly opened, maybe that day. What is more amazing, Mrs Hooper checked with every family member, asking if they'd visited the graveyard recently. None had. The last call was three months ago. Therefore, no one belonging to Antony had any knowledge of the flower. And that was the first time I'd ever been to that place. In fact, if you asked me to go back now, I wouldn't know the way.

We were all greatly impressed by Antony's ingenuity. He'd not only proved his existence, but foxed the psychic researchers who say mediums read people's minds. He had beaten them all — and very cleverly — with one solitary daisy.

Weeks later, when I suddenly saw a red jumper with a broken seam floating near Mrs Hooper, she recognized it as her son's. So, grabbing paper and pen, I quickly scribbled down this letter from him to his mother:

I'm very happy where I am, and am in touch with all the family by thought. I've withdrawn my presence because now I've almost mastered the ability to register thoughts, as my previous list of evidential statements proves.

I'm living in a sort of small flat. It's great! I don't have to clean up after me at all!

I wasn't in the church tonight, and I'm very aware of what you were supposed to have received from me. I'm sorry, Mum, but I didn't transmit a thing.'

This remark refers to a message Mrs Hooper was given by a 'medium' that night. Antony goes on:

I do know how difficult it's been for you on times since I went. As I remember my last few hours, I know it was a stupid thing to do. In drink, no one's in their right senses really.

I'm not present in the room. My thought waves reach down often as they do now. I want you to know I'm safe. Information can always come down to you about which you know nothing.

Did my daisy surprise you? Hope so.

I've been with Nanny Hooper recently. We've shared some lovely times together. I haven't got any solid evidence to transmit tonight, more of a friendly, kind note to let you know how I am.

My leg doesn't hurt any more — this new body's great! And I've grown a few inches and my hair has darkened a bit.

Mrs Hooper recalled he'd broken his leg 18 months before he died, and his hair was lightened when here. Antony finishes:

Love to Dad. I love you all, Antony . . . Will be in touch again, but will pick my mediums carefully. No dopey ones!

And, true to his word, Antony Hooper, the young lad who was killed by the midnight train, has returned dozens of times to his family. He's even rapped walls and furniture in his mother's home in answer to questions. Time and again, he's returned to prove his survival.

Other mediums have often brought him to me. They name him and add: 'He says you are his friend.' And so I am. But I never knew him on earth; he is a messenger.

I can do no better than close with a letter from Mrs Hooper; if you have lost a child, her words may bring you hope and comfort:

To all mothers who have lost children, I would say: Your child is not dead, but still alive.

Don't believe they're at rest, because they're not.

Don't believe that they have gone for ever, because they have not.

And I know through good mediumship, with patience and determination to keep on searching, you will find them again.

Rain Pools

Rain Pools,
Rain Pools,
Watering the ground;
Splish splash
Rain Pools,
Water all around.

Snowflakes,
Whiteflakes,
Floating on the air;
Pirouetting Earthward,
Watch the children stare.

Grey hail,
Dark hail,
Bouncing off the pane;
'Look, Mum!'
'Yes, John,
It's only frozen rain.'

'Sleep, John.
Rest now,
It's been a tiring day.'
'Right, Mum.
Night Mum.'
And soon he's on his way.

As Johnathan sleeps,
His mother weeps,
Unable to understand
Why the one she loves more than life itself,
Must soon slip from her hand.

'See the X-Rays,'
The doctor said.
'There isn't any doubt.
Your little boy is dying,
And time is running out.'

Rain Pools,
Rain Pools,
Johnny's favourite sound;
Splish splash
Rain Pools,
Watering the ground.

Summer came
As Winter left,
And little boys grew tall;
All, that is, bar Johnathan French,
Who, too weak to move,
Too frail to breathe,
Daily lost his strength.

John's fragile frame grew smaller
As each day came and went.
His body became thin,
His face drew in
Till all his fight was spent.

'Mum, the sun is shining!
Take me to the window, please?
Just ignore what the doctor says,
I want to see the sun again,
I want to feel the breeze.
I want to watch the raindrops
Splashing on the ground,
Making little Rain Pools —
That's my favourite sound.'

So Johnny's Mum
Lifts up her son,
And carries him to the light.
And her tears fall, so quietly,
Hidden from his sight.
(Such a kind boy,
Such a good boy;
It doesn't make sense at all.
He's done no wrong,
He's far too young,
Too innocent and small.)

(Just eight years old,
And he won't see nine,
Or ever know a wife;
He wants to watch the raindrops fall,
Please God, spare his life.)

(Let my son be well again,
Give *me* what ails him so.
It's fit that I should end my time:
Spare John, and let *me* go.)

But God, it seems, was busy;
For He didn't heed her cry.
And from Beyond He called John's name:
And little Johnathan died ...

Rain Pools,
Rain Pools,
Watering the ground;
Splish splash
Rain Pools,
Johnny's favourite sound.

And there in a dusty graveyard,
Kneeling all forlorn,
Is an aching grief-stricken mother,
Her wrecked life shattered and torn:
'John, I've come to see you again,
It's so hard to forget your pain.
But it's better that you're at peace, my son,
Than to have suffered and remained.'

'Daddy loves you, darling,
And Susie's tears still fall;
And all your friends still think of you, John:
But I miss you most of all.'

And she places her eight red roses tall,
One per year of his life
(Which blossomed and now is run)
And her constant tears incessantly fall,
Making little Rain Pools
On the grave of her special son.

Rain Pools,
Rain Pools,
Watering the ground;

Splish splash
Rain Pools;
John still hears the sound . . .

11

Animals Survive Too

It was pitch-black night. The car sped along the motorway lit only by a few pools of orange glow here and there. Then suddenly from out of the shadows shot a black cat. It pelted across the dark road keeping close to the ground and increasing its speed as it flew past the front of the car. But we were moving too quickly. There was a scream from underneath the passenger wheel and the whole car jolted as it ran over the animal's body.

We stopped about 100 yards up the road. I flung the door open and in a frenzied panic I ran back along the road, dodging traffic as I went. The dark patch of shuddering animal on the tarmac came nearer and nearer, and then I was right beside the victim. The poor cat was bleeding from a cracked skull. Its eyes were wide open and staring, its mouth pulled right back in terror. As we watched the last throes of life ebbing away we felt so utterly helpless. But it wasn't our fault. Before we knew what had happened it was under the wheel. A pure accident.

Suddenly the cat stretched and shuddered. And then I knew its spirit was trying to break loose from its body. As I watched, the spirit freed itself and the cat's lifeless form contracted before my eyes. Its spirit dashed across the road into the nearby bushes and freedom. That was the first time I'd ever been involved in the killing of an animal, and it was an horrendous experience.

We stood there both deeply ashamed, my driver and I, shocked and full of regret. We took a shovel and dug a grave for the body at the road-side grassland. Frantically at 2.30 am we scratched and scrabbled at the earth to give the cat a decent burial.

'Do you want to say a few words?' I asked my driver. And I left him there while I tidied up the roadway. When I glanced back he was bitterly crying with shock and remorse.

When I reported the incident to the police the officer wasn't interested. 'It's only a reportable offence if it's a dog,' he said chirpily.

'We're not one bit interested in your traffic rules,' I retorted. 'We're concerned about the feelings of the cat's owners should they contact you.'

I've always loved animals and since childhood I've been aware of a spiritual kinship with them. When I was a small boy we kept two chickens which laid fresh eggs almost every day, and it was such a thrill to collect them straight from the hutch. After a few years, however, the grown-ups decided they would be killed and prepared for the table. Horrified and incensed, I pleaded for their lives. What harm had they ever done? Why should they be destroyed and eaten? But, shout as I might, no one listened to me and a friend's husband was called in to do the unpleasant job.

Mr Morgan was a coarse, unfeeling man and, to me, he relished the thought of his task. But I don't think he'd bargained for my opposition when he arrived. I stood against the back door barring his exit to the garden.

'Come on, son, clear out of the way,' he snarled.

'No,' I exclaimed, bracing myself against the door jambs. 'I won't let you near them! You're not going to kill them! They've never hurt anyone and I won't let you do it!'

But I'm afraid I was too small and puny to be a bodily threat and he brushed me aside like a feather and marched out into the garden, a sharp knife glinting in his hand. I pulled madly at the door, but he'd locked it from outside. Awkwardly, I clambered onto a stool and craned my neck to see through the window. Pummelling the glass, I screamed out again and again to save their lives. But with a boorish idiotic smirk, and a few twists of his hands, their necks were broken before my horrified gaze.

I ran upstairs in a frenzy and cried and sobbed for hours. 'Why do people have to be so cruel?' I kept asking myself.

Later, our chickens were both plucked, cleaned and made ready for the table, but I wouldn't touch them. I point-blankly refused. The whole episode had made me feel sick inside, and on that day I fully realized many people didn't care about our fellow creatures, the animals.

Many owners are distressed when their beloved pets die and they're eager to know if their friends have survived death. I can happily report that they do. I've lost count of the times spirit animals have returned to their masters and mistresses through my mediumship. In most cases they bring a feeling of warmth and gratitude for the concern and love shown to them when on earth. Where animals have been loved and have shared a close bond with us they have been helped into a greater awareness of their own individuality, which assures their survival and return. Even creatures other than our domestic pets live on into eternity.

At a Yorkshire meeting an elderly miner returned to his niece in the audience with some good news. Uncle Ernie asked her: 'How's it going, lass?'

'Tell him I'm fine,' she called out.

'Good,' he replied to me. 'Eh, you'll never guess who I've got over here wi' me, lass? Remember old Nellie and Jessie?'

'Oh, yes!' exclaimed his neice. 'They were the two pit-ponies he took care of down the mines.'

'That's them,' he returned, and added: 'Can you remember, lass, they were down't pit so long that when they retired t'surface, they were both blind as bats.'

'Yes, I do remember,' she said. 'He loved them as though they were his own two children.'

At this Uncle Ernie beamed and called out joyously to me: 'Well lass, I still love 'em I do! And what do you think? They can both see now.' And when I looked around the hall nearly everyone's eyes had misted up.

But horses were not the only deceased pets to pay me a visit while working. During a question-and-answer session at Pembroke the audience began to look at me strangely. They couldn't understand why I kept grinning and scrutinizing the air above their heads. What they didn't know was I could see a bright blue-and-green spirit budgerigar dive-bombing the crowd and flying high up into the rafters again! It was such a comical sight and so real a vision that for a moment I thought he'd got in through an open window. Eventually I had to tell everyone what was happening and as soon as I did, he flew from the top of the hall right down onto my shoulder. I could feel his little claws digging into my skin (my spirit-body skin, of course). Then a woman appeared and took him onto her finger. She relayed a successful message to her relative present, saying: 'I've got Edgar with me.'

'Oh, I'm so glad. He only died a few days ago and I've been so worried about him.' But there was nothing to fear, for he was still very much alive and chirruping away, swearing as he did on earth!

Another happy return of a much-loved pet was that of my beautiful chinchilla rabbit, Smokey. I kept her when I was 14. She was slate grey, a cuddly, fluffy ball of fun and fur, and very affectionate too. Every time I entered the shed where she lived she'd come hopping over to greet me and sniff at my pockets to see if I'd brought her fresh food. But sadly, after a week's illness, Smokey died. Tearfully, I buried her body in the garden. I missed her terribly. When I cleaned out the shed I found hundreds of teeth-marks in the wood where she used to sharpen her ever-growing incisors.

A few days passed by and then one morning while sitting in the lounge, reading, I felt something pulling at my shoe. When I looked down there was no one there. All I could see was the sole of my shoe being physically tugged and gnawed. And in that instant I knew Smokey had returned. She'd never been allowed in the house before but her love for me and her desire to be near me brought her to my side. How marvellous to know that even our lesser brethren survive. Or are they lesser? When I look at their gentle behaviour and loyal trust and then measure this against man, I sometimes wonder who is the more evolved.

Perhaps the most unusual creatures to make contact came at a Staffordshire meeting. Can you imagine my astonishment when a fully-grown Indian elephant appeared in the aisle? I took a deep breath and ventured a description.

'I'm not getting a name,' I said, which tickled the audience, 'but I do see a distinctively-dressed Indian boy looking after him.' Then I described the young lad in detail.

'Here!' called out a man near the front. It turned out that he had been a game-keeper in India, and fully recognized the spirit-lad and also the elephant. 'Thank Goodness for that,' I thought. I was quite relieved, because just behind the elephant I could see a giraffe coming into view! 'Oh well, if he's taken the one, he's bound to accept the other,' I thought. So I sallied forth with the giraffe, to which he replied: 'Yes. I can take two actually.' Everyone fell about laughing and boggled their minds, wondering how on earth I was going to sort it out! But instead I simply said: 'Well I don't know which one we've got here, they all look alike to me. But it's the one that was close to the elephant.'

'Ah, yes!' he shrilled out. 'I perfectly understand' — much to the amusement of the crowd.

In contrast, it was an emotional, touching moment when a blind man warmly accepted a golden labrador guide-dog from the spirit-world. Even though death had separated them, Sandy, his first guide-dog, sat quietly beside him, attracted by undying love and loyalty, reminding us that bonds of friendship can never be broken — not even by death.

People have often asked me over the years if pets are psychic: the answer is 'yes'. Animals' minds are uncluttered and free of prejudice and social etiquette. Even the most humble of pets possess a soul-ability of sensing or seeing spirit-people that most of us find difficult to register.

I used to visit a large pet shop in an open market, regularly feeling sorry for the caged creatures and tanked fish. It must be a far from ideal life for them, all cooped up in those confined spaces. I know we wouldn't like it. We put people in small places like that as a punishment. But what have the animals done?

In one of the tanks lived a black-and-white Moray Eel. And whenever I approached his place his psychic sense immediately knew I was near. He'd come to the front of the tank to greet me before he could actually see me nearby. That's because we'd struck up a kind of unusual friendship, I guess.

'Hello,' I'd whisper. 'Still here then? Never mind, someone'll come along and give you a good home. You'll see.' And whatever people may say or think, that Moray Eel 'knew' what I was saying, because he seemed to settle down after that. Then one rainy day when I called on my friend — he'd gone. I really hope he got a kind owner.

Animals psychically know instinctively when they are safe or in danger. And Woody was no exception. He was a wild pigeon who used to perch on my bedroom window-sill for years. He'd rest peacefully on one leg with his head tucked underneath his wing. These timid creatures normally need a long association with people before they gain our trust, but Woody psychically sensed that he was quite safe with me. No matter how many lights were flicked off and on or how many doors were banged in the early hours, Woody never flinched. A part of his spirit was able to reach out and touch a part of mine and he knew beyond doubt that no harm would come to him at my house. This soul-power or psychic power is resident in every living thing, and animals in particular are extremely sensitive beings. They can register human emotions because their psychic abilities operate freely, and I fervently believe that they, like us, are spirits working through physical bodies.

Our faithful cat and my childhood companion, Tibby, went out one night and sadly never returned. Eventually we got word that a school caretaker had found her killed on the road. It was a sad goodbye to a lovely friend. She was a remarkable cat. She used to walk my mother down to the shops, sit at the kerb until the traffic was clear and then walk my mother over safely. Only then would she go off and play. There's no doubt about it, I am a cat man.

While taking a meeting in aid of the Eighton Banks Animal Sanctuary I was moved to read a banner hanging high above the platform at the Concorde Centre, Washington. On it was written: 'If you show kindness to these my lesser brethren, you have shown kindness unto me'.

The meeting went well and afterwards was followed by a delicious home-baked vegetarian feast (to show any carnivores present an alternative way of titillating the palate without cruelty to animals). Then, from the animal sanctuary, I became the proud owner of Sooty, a grey and white female cat. She walks like John Wayne, is into everything, bossy and very independent. We've grown to love one another greatly and she won't let anyone tickle her stomach except me.

Sooty loves company, which is why she kept bounding in and out of my bed at night. In the end I couldn't sleep until I placed her basket outside on the landing and firmly locked the door. Yet her spirit was not a bit deterred. In the middle of the night I'd be rudely awoken by her four feet pounding over the duvet. I could feel her full body-weight pressing down on me. And it was only after I'd 'thrown' her off with my feet that I dozily realized she wasn't in the room at all. Her physical body was sound asleep on the landing outside and in her spirit-counterpart she'd walked right through the locked door and bothered me again! This became a nightly occurrence. The same process repeated itself time and again, until one night . . .

As well as Sooty's spirit feet bouncing on the sheets there was also another tight ball of fear crouched close to my left knee. There were *two* animals in the bed, both in their spirit-forms. Before I had time to be perplexed, the sensations faded away. But everything soon became clear when Keith and Elizabeth — two exceptionally spiritual people — rang to plead: 'Will you take another cat from the sanctuary?' But how could I? Sooty was enough of a handful on her own!

A few days later Keith arrived on my doorstep with Bess. She turned out to be the 'frightened ball of fear' I'd psychically felt huddled next to my leg several nights previously. I can only assume the spirit-people had brought her. When I finally prised Bess out of her box, she dived into my arms, buried her head in my jumper and stayed there for three solid hours without moving.

Down in the music room I massaged her tight neck to reduce her tension and fear, and after 45 minutes she suddenly began to purr like a train! After that she spent three days in her own basket, still petrified. The sanctuary had told me she'd never seen a home before so I suppose it was understandable. No one could approach without her burying her head in her blanket.

When she eventually did settle in, she took a few brave steps out of her box and Sooty thought she was live target practice! She pounced on top of her and wrestled her to the floor, pinning her down by the neck triumphantly. Another victory for John Wayne!

I'd already been told by the sanctuary that I should return Bess if I couldn't cope. And after a while I could see their point. I began to despair, thinking she'd never feel at home with me. Then while walking out one day, pondering about Bess's future, I clearly heard a voice inside my head say, 'Please love the cat.' On the strength of this, I kept her. And I was so glad I had. Just as soon as she felt at ease, she turned out to be a real lady — not at all like Sooty. Bess had a quiet, gentle personality, in absolute contrast to Sooty's wicked mischief.

They soon got along fine; they went everywhere together and were inseparable, two great pals. They'd clean each other's coats and twirl around each other, cuddling up on cold nights to keep out the draughts. They were a smashing team.

But I didn't realize what that voice had really meant when it begged me to keep Bess. As time went on, her behaviour started to change. One day I scolded her for not using her litter box. It was her second accident. It was then I noticed something was wrong. She'd always wobbled a little and swaggered when she walked — in fact friends nicknamed her 'Wobbler'. But on this day she positively reeled from side to side against the walls, into the furniture. It was then I knew why she hadn't used her litter tray — it was down on the lower landings and Bess couldn't manage to descend the stairs without pain.

I rushed her to the People's Dispensary for Sick Animals and they diagnosed a possible brain tumour and meningitis, an inflammation of the brain membranes. After this, Bess deteriorated slowly over several months. The special antibiotics only brought temporary relief. She was falling in and out of blindness, was incontinent, and had no sense of balance at all. For three months I nursed her like a baby. I'd made her a special waterproof bed, and lined it with old newspapers, but poor Bess was failing fast.

I taught her to walk again, overcoming the paralysis in her hind limbs completely, but then she fell extremely ill. She would call out in desperate pain, so frustrated and unable to find any relief from the agony she suffered.

On Sunday night, I knelt by her basket and closed my eyes and prayed. I asked that if she was to be taken across to the spirit-world the next day at the PDSA, that my grandfather would be near to receive her and care for her. I instinctively felt it would be her last night on earth and as I finished the prayer I could sense my spirit-friends moving away. They had received the message.

At the vet's they advised that because she was in such great distress and because her personality had changed into a violent frustrated one, she should be put to sleep. I was stunned and silent. A lump came into my throat as I nervously signed the paper for them, against my better judgement.

'I want to be with her,' I said in a whisper. They agreed, and they cut some fur from her front paw and prepared the injection.

'Will she feel any pain?' I asked.

'No. It's an overdose of barbiturates. It'll be instantaneous.'

'She mustn't feel any pain,' I quietly said again.

'Don't worry, she won't.' From somewhere a nurse appeared and helped to gently smoothe Bess, who gave a little trembling stretch.

'Lie still, sweetheart,' she said. 'There's a good girl.' I bent down and kissed her.

'Shh,' I whispered. 'Goodbye, Bess, safe journey.' And then the injection was given.

Her eyes opened fully. Her heart stopped beating. And Bess was gone.

Tears streamed down my face as I kissed her and smoothed her fine coat. I was so upset. I left clutching my empty box, pushing my way through a full waiting-room to people's sympathetic sighs. I was shaking, crying and shocked. I'd taken Bess in good faith and she'd trusted me to help her, and then I'd signed a form for them to take her life.

I couldn't speak. I couldn't catch the bus home. I walked all the way, uncontrollably sobbing and tearful. When I got home, I collapsed onto a chair and broke my heart. How could I have made that decision? How could I live with myself after that? I felt so terribly guilty; I'd never forgive myself. And I still don't. Even though people said it was the right thing to do, the heavy burden of guilt lingers with me to this day. I'd killed her, just as surely as if I'd given the injection myself.

Sooty and I missed Bess terribly that winter. Sooty would sit on the landing staring at her empty box, sighing. Then she'd look across at me as if to say, 'When is she coming back?' I sat at the piano and composed a piece of music in tribute to our friend and called it 'Gentle Bess'.

Then, one night, as Sooty and I sat quietly in the music room I heard Bess cry out from beyond the door out on the landing. Sooty sat bolt upright. She'd heard it too. Then there was scratching at the wood from outside.

I dashed across and opened the door. I couldn't see Bess but I sensed her walking in, swaggering along. Sooty ran over and greeted her, sniffing the air and happily playing with her friend and companion. Sooty's happy face was a picture.

A little while later, while sitting in meditation, my spirit-vision opened up and I could see Bess in the spirit-world seated in a patch of sunlight under some flowering bushes. She always did love warmth. Behind her the house door opened and out stepped my grandfather. He was much younger than when he had died and he went over to Bess and stroked her fine coat with loving hands. Then he raised his head and smiled at me. And I couldn't help marvelling at the power of thought and the power of love. How mighty they both are.

My prayer had been answered. Bess had arrived safely on the Other Side, no longer in any pain and completely free of disease. Furthermore she was under the loving care of my grandfather — just as I'd asked.

The Voiceless Ones

Voiceless Ones
The Voiceless Ones,
Who will hear the cry of
The Voiceless Ones?

Fighting Fish;
Wrenched by your mouth
From the deep —
Killed —
And served up in a dish.

Gentle Sheep;
Stolen from your mother,
And pushed along an aisle of death,
Too afraid to weep.

Featherless Chicken;
Standing on wires,
Laying eggs for man,

Who'll cook your bones
And pick them.

Turkeys, Ducks and Geese;
Will killings ever cease?
Still slaughtered in your millions
To praise a Prince of Peace.

Voiceless Ones
The Voiceless Ones,
Who will hear the cry of
The Voiceless Ones?

Frightened Fox;
Chased for sporting blood,
Or caught in a gin-trap
That cracks your limbs and locks.

Majestic Giant Whale;
Killed by a spear
Through your brain,
Then turned into cosmetics
For profitable sale.

Monkeys; Dogs; Birds and Cats;
Seals and Calves; Mice and Rats;
Imprisoned by Science:
Electrically jolted,
Shaved and moulted;
Fastened to contraptions,
Strapped and bolted:
Cannot move,
Cannot rest;
Unspeakable cruelty
In the name of progress.

Skins for fashion,
Furs for clothes,
Meats for the belly
Bludgeoned by blows.
When will it cease?
When man knows that all these creatures
Are friends not foes.

No need for meat;
There's much to eat:
Fruit, nuts, plants, and others —
And lest we forget:
Man is also an animal,
And animals are our brothers.

And it's foolish to think
This has nothing to do with you,
For you contribute too:
Whenever you buy meat,
Fur coats, cosmetics,
Or leather shoes.

Thoughtless man —
Put away your guns,
And pity the cry of
The Voiceless Ones.

12

Psychic Powers

The telephone rang. 'Would you come and see us, Mr O'Brien? Our radio station's haunted.'

Well, it was one of the strangest requests I'd received. How could I resist it?

I was interviewed at about 11.30 at night and then I was to conduct the séance at around midnight. I told the presenters that time was irrelevant, but it didn't seem to matter to them. However, after my live talk on the air the switchboards jammed as usual. But I didn't know that then; I was creeping down a dimly lit corridor with a reporter creeping behind me armed with a cassette recorder.

'I won't tell you where they say it is,' she confided secretly.

'No need,' I replied. 'It's right here.' And the air was chill all about that spot. I couldn't answer any more of her questions, because I could see a form gliding into the energy fields about me. She was a kindly-looking soul, wearing an old-fashioned long grey nurse's uniform, or what looked like one. She carried a bucket of clean water, rolls of bandages and a wad of clean rags.

The reporter peered into the dimness, checking her watch as midnight approached, but she couldn't see the vision that transfixed my gaze. The nurse of long ago bent down close to the ground which was below the current level of the radio station corridor floor. Then just as she neared the tiles, a soldier came into my sight. He was dying, taking his last breath; and I psychically sensed him calling out for her aid. She wiped his brow with her cloths, and tended to his wounds. So great was the emotion of gratitude emanating from him and the feelings of pity radiating from her that my eyes filled up with compassion for these two who were no longer of our world. This pair of apparitions of centuries ago instantly struck my senses with the information that they were not real spirit-people making a visitation, but they were energy pictures caught up in the atmosphere.

Then I was interviewed.

'She comes along this corridor,' I said, 'and is seen just here where this chilly spot is in the psychic atmosphere.'

'That's perfectly correct,' retorted my baffled companion. 'This is where the sightings have occurred.'

'I think if you'll check,' I went on, 'I sense this was the place of a particularly bloody battle centuries ago. In fact I can feel many conflicts have occurred here on this ground. Your "Lady in Grey" was a nurse of sorts tending to the wounded and dying. I feel she was allowed to walk amongst the injured without harm. When she approached a dying soldier just here,' and I indicated the exact spot, 'the powerful emotions released in them both blended and "pictured" them in the atmosphere, the psychic energy fields. So your ghost is not a living, communicating entity. She's a picture from the past.'

The reporter was visibly impressed, replying: 'I can reveal now that historical records sight this as a battle-ground in centuries gone, several battles were fought here actually. That's amazing, Stephen.'

I don't know if they saw their Lady in Grey again. I think they probably did. But anyhow, she wouldn't harm them. How could she? She was only a psychic snapshot.

This kind of sensitivity was quietly building up within me and heralded a new area of my psychic work. Mediums can use their own soul-powers or psychic energies to register vibrations of sight, sense and sound which don't necessarily reach us from the spirit-world, as in the above case. I wasn't contacting the

Other Side when I saw the Lady in Grey; it was purely an exercise of my own psychic powers.

Instead of directing my sensitivity towards the spirit-realms beyond, I channelled it a little nearer to home. This psychic sensitivity can bring some startling results when correctly used. And I'm quite sure many people are aware of it operating in their own lives.

One area I can use these soul-powers in is the reading of auras. The aura is an electromagnetic field of swirling energies which encompasses all things living and inanimate. Much research has been done on it in recent years which has proved that sensitives have not only seen it, but correctly described it in accurate detail. In fact there are seveal auras in existence around people and objects, but they mostly blend to form what looks like a sort of translucent soap-bubble of rainbow colours — ever changing, ever moving, and vibrant. The aura can hold within its magnetic fields all kinds of interesting information, as I soon discovered . . .

A lecturer once approached me to use my sensitivity in an unusual, constructive way. He was responsible for dozens of students under his care. But one of them, he felt, was responsible for the mystifying letters he'd been receiving anonymously. They were of a disturbing sexual nature and certainly indicated that their sender was in need of professional, medical care. Could I help? I said I'd try.

Present before a class of 40 students, none of whom knew I was undertaking this experiment, I extended my auric fields and embraced the students within my powers. Then, using my clairvoyant ability, I carefully scanned each one, quietly and privately one by one, until there in the electromagnetic fields of light around one student I found the telling information. Clairvoyantly I could see the selfsame details contained in the letters hovering in the mind of the sender. I privately named the student and my findings were later proved correct.

Sensitives can read the entire life-story of objects by becoming attuned to the vibrational fields around them. Of course, we sometimes interpret the visions incorrectly, but nevertheless we can be successful.

On a sightseeing trip to a museum a friend and I decided to tune in to the mummified remains of an Egyptian priest, Tem-Hor. This kind of exercise is known as psychometry. Placing our hands on the glass cabinet, we moved our minds towards the lifeless mummy. Even though the last earthly impressions of his life were put into the vibrational fields of this Priest of Isis about 220 BC, more than 2,000 years ago, we got a scant picture of his life.

Between us, Graeme and I saw this man moving through rich hanging draperies in a magnificent palace, and being consulted by Royalty. The colours were glowing, the palace beautifully ornate and decorated with gold and precious gems. Then I saw Tem-Hor sitting at some kind of desk, writing on clay and parchment, probably papyrus. As I watched, I felt the awful sensation of cold metal thrusting into my back with a deadening thud. He was murdered.

Graeme saw the ritual funeral procession, getting the feeling he wasn't considered an important man and the proceedings were undertaken out of quick necessity rather than out of love. Then the impressions faded and we stood once more in the cold museum, being eyed conspicuously by a warden.

Another interesting reading I did was given when I was handed a peculiarly-shaped stone. I clasped it tightly to me and began to register sensations immediately. The link was so strong, so very real, that as I relayed my impressions I spoke as though I was the voice of the rock.

'I'm in a wall or part of a castle. I can smell gunpowder smoke and hear the cries of dying men. Just down the grassy bank there are swans on the moat; they're fleeing from the noise in terror. There is thunder in the dark skies above me . . .

'Now the rain comes. I can feel it bouncing off my surface, cooling me after the hot sun.' Then the scenes shifted as I tuned in to another part of its past.

'The clash of metal is all around me and those cries of pain are here again. There are men dying and dead on the grassy banks, some of them are calling out in agony and giving up the spirit. I can hear canons firing and a spear has just glanced off my surface. Oh God, someone's being killed up against my vision . . . blood is splattering all over my sight . . . '

Then quickly my mind dismissed these impressions and found another area to view. 'That scene passes now, thank God, and I can see a small campfire flickering on the grasses. It is night. The air is cold but stilled. The battle's over I think. It finished days ago. And these men I see have been clearing the ground of dead and any treasures they wanted. They're gently singing songs and drinking ale. I think they're pleased with their day's work. One of them, a big chap, is sneering and tossing gold coins in the air. He's taken these from one of the dead.' And then I tuned out and back into the present-day room.

The researcher explained that the piece of rock had been prised from the walls of an ancient castle which had seen many battles. It was taken from the wall at about a man's height, overlooking a dry grassy slope which would have once been a moat.

Isn't it amazing that so-called 'dead' objects can photograph and capture for all time sights and sounds they've experienced? It makes me fully accept what the Red Indians believe, particularly White Owl my Guardian Spirit. Many times he's said: 'You think you have so much knowledge, but indeed today's civilization has lost many of the great truths known to man in the past. We knew, the people of my race, that what seems lifeless to the slow, heavy senses of the flesh is not without life at all. It has its own consciousness, its own specialized form of spirit awareness. To you the dead rocks and stones are immovable and of no great consequence to mankind. Yet they exist through time much longer than man's puny physical frame. The rocks have their own lives to lead. They move over the centuries. They breathe the great breath of the Spirit. How foolish is man to assume he is the epitome of all growth. He will one day retrace his steps back to the ancient wisdoms he has so conveniently forgotten.'

White Owl has often told us that he himself was a medium when on earth and he 'read' the plants and stones. When people or objects were lost, the Red Indians — those who were sufficiently gifted and trained — could 'ask' the countryside if it had seen the missing articles or people. The same method was used, just as in the above case. White Owl is always fascinating to listen to when he speaks of his past.

The word *psychometry* comes from the Greek. Literally translated it can be split up into two sections: *Psyche* (meaning Soul) and *Metron* (meaning to Measure). Psychometry, then, means the process whereby we can 'measure the soul of things'.

To prove that this works, however, we need some feedback of facts which can be verified beyond doubt; and I've done this on numerous occasions. A good example was when I was suddenly called out onto the platform by Gordon Higginson, Principal of a College of Psychic Studies, who unexpectedly blindfolded me. Without warning Gordon thrust an object into my hand and said, 'Stephen will now psychometrize this ring.'

I then began rattling off facts and details about its owner, having made the psychic connection through the article. The ring had become a kind of 'key' which opened the doorway to the spirit to whom it belonged. Actually, I found out later it was the property of a Mrs Judd from Portsmouth. She was a rather jolly lady of considerable proportions. That's why the whole audience giggled and tittered when I confidently announced: 'Whoever owns this can tap-dance.' I guess the mental picture of Mrs Judd tripping the light fantastic had titillated them.

But back came Gordon's answer to me: 'Yes, when she was younger.' He didn't allow the recipient to speak in case her identity out of the 80 students that week would be revealed. I went on.

'This person is worried about some documentation she's gathered together specially to present a case of some kind. I feel she has the papers with her and intends to make her case known.'

All this was accepted with a 'yes'. But afterwards she explained that in her possession that very afternoon she had signed affidavits from 26 persons about a legal matter she intended to bring to the attention of lawyers. The whole audience gasped when I loudly pronounced: 'And whoever the owner is she — because it is a woman — has a strong link to Portsmouth.' Mrs Judd lived there.

Several people have asked me to use my psychic powers to help them. One was an eminent healer.

'Stephen,' she asked, 'have a look at one of my patients for me will you? See what you can see with him.' I agreed, and tuned into the chap sitting across the way who was having healing from two smart ladies. I didn't like the feelings he was carrying within him. Despite the fact that he was outwardly serene something else was lurking in the dark background of his character. Afterwards I privately relayed my impressions to the healing group leader.

'As well as being deeply in grief . . .'

'Yes, he's recently lost his wife,' I was informed.

'. . . I'm afraid he's thoroughly enjoying the closeness and touch of your female healers.'

'That's exactly what I'd suspected,' she replied. We agreed it would be a good idea to next week give him a gentleman as a healer in a bid to stem these unwanted feelings which could only have caused him concern if they continued.

The next week he was healed by a man. And the week after that he didn't return. Of course, the healing group continued sending him help through the spirit-world, but I don't think they saw him at the session again.

Many people have come to me in dire distress seeking aid. And although they freely speak their thoughts they don't always tell the truth. Or they withold information which they feel might make them look silly. Such a case was the woman who claimed that all manner of psychic disturbances were bothering her. She claimed she was followed by a 'dead' man who wouldn't go away from her and questioned her incessantly. But something was not as it seemed.

Private investigation into the auric fields about her revealed, as she was busy speaking, that within her was a history of mental illness. As she chatted away, I also sent a thought to White Owl for help. His observations confirmed mine exactly: 'She is still mentally unbalanced,' he said. 'Be very careful and as tactful as possible.'

I gently questioned her about medical help. At first she thoroughly denied she had been ill, but later she reluctantly admitted it. We helped her as much as we could.

At the time of writing it's against British law for anyone to diagnose illnesses unless they are a qualified doctor. So whenever I've done this it's always been to closed groups of students and willing participators who understand something of psychic power and who aren't vulnerable to the power of suggestion.

I called out a lady and read her auric field concentrating particularly on the physical aura emanating about an inch or so in depth all about the body. In it are contained all our health problems.

'I see three difficulties here. There are shadows on your left ankle, the right kidney and at the top of your neck.'

The lady replied: 'I broke my left ankle last year, I'm under supervision for kidney problems and I've been diagnosed last week as having osteo-arthritis in my neck.' The audience needn't have gasped — it was all in her auric fields for anyone who had developed the power to perceive it.

I'm sure many people have experienced certain psychic feelings, just like me; those inexplicable sensations of going into a room full of smiling, happy people and yet you 'know' there's just been a raging argument in that place. That's our auric field registering the true condition.

Our perceptions can be *wrong* of course, and we must never ever deceive ourselves into thinking we are right *all* the time, because we are not. It takes years of careful development to perfect these skills and even now I can still get it wrong. I was spot-on however when Kenny, an officious under-manager where I worked, smiled a sickly smile and said: 'The Top Management want you to do some overtime at the weekend, Stephen. How about it?'

I looked him right in the eye, annoyed at his bumptious behaviour over the previous few weeks, and replied firmly: 'That's a lie. The Management want *you* to do it and you want to coax *me* to take your place.'

The poor chap was dumbstruck. I'd read his secret, and Kenny never bothered with me much after that.

Sometimes I'd get the most peculiar feeling that someone was calling to me, just as though people in *this* world, not the next, were wishing to see me, hear from me, or have a contact with me. One week I kept getting thoughts or calls from Mrs Scott who lived hundreds of miles away in Cheltenham. I hadn't seen her for ages but kept feeling I should telephone. So at the end of a nagging week, I dialled her number.

'Oh hello, Stephen. How lovely to hear your voice! It's a wonder your ears aren't dropping off — I've been talking about you all week.' She went on to say that it was the anniversary of her husband's passing and that she'd been feeling a little low. Obviously her thoughts had reached out and touched me.

Speaking of the telephone, I got rather good at knowing who was on the other end when it rang. That was extremely useful, particularly if it was someone very trying on days when I wasn't up to scratch. Friends didn't believe me when I told them. 'Pick it up then,' I'd challenge them, 'and see if I'm right.' And nearly always, I was.

Being a psychic sensitive and a medium I was called on to make investigations that others may have run a hundred miles from in the opposite direction. One such event was at Barrhead, a suburb of Glasgow. I was taken to a small terraced house.

There's definitely something awful in here,' confided my trembling hostess. 'Take a look about.' So armed with youthful pluck and a knowledge that White Owl was close at hand in all my psychic efforts I wandered through the humble rooms. There was positively nothing downstairs. But as I climbed the staircase I could feel the emanations of a powerful dark force. Unfortunately I whispered out to myself, 'By the pricking of my thumbs something evil this way comes,' not realizing that half of the party with me heard it and fled out into the street.

As I approached the upper rooms I sensed nothing untoward in two of them, but when I neared the third door I knew I'd struck gold. I was just about to say to my hostess 'It's in here', but her strained expression told me not to bother; I was right.

Furtively, I opened the bedroom door and felt the most awful sickly sensation of utter hatred I'd ever experienced. I went to take a step into the room but I bumped into a solid wall of psychic power. I was visibly thrown back a few feet.

'Oh God,' she said, 'that happens to me too.'

Undaunted, I marched across to the doorway again and just as I was about to thrust myself through it — it suddenly slammed tight shut in my face.

'I don't think we're welcome here,' I murmured feebly. So down the stairs we trouped and had a cup of tea and a chat about 'him up there'.

I was convinced someone from the Other Side had taken up residence in that bedroom and a few quick words with White Owl confirmed it. 'I'll remove him,' he said. 'He's too strong for your world to do this. He's nearer to us than you. Leave it with me and I'll deal with it properly.' And so we did as he asked. Shortly after this the hostess heard some scuffling from that bedroom, and after that silence reigned. The 'heavy brigade' had gone in and taken 'him up there' away.

Another unworldly visitor, only this time not a malicious one, made himself known through my psychic sensitivity one evening while I was having supper in an eighteenth-century farmhouse in Glyncorrwg, Wales. The house was a beautiful place, full of history and oaken beams across the ceiling and walls.

While supping my tea, all at once I heard the sound of heavy footsteps dragging along above the ceiling. I kept quiet about it for a while but then it came again. I looked up.

'What's the matter with you?' asked my friend.

'Oh, there's a man walking above us,' I said glibly, 'and he's got really *huge* feet. He keeps dragging them along, scraping the floorboards. I can hear him, can't you?' And she couldn't.

The sound disappeared out into a bedroom and then into thin air. There was no room where I could still hear his steps, just a kind of old attic area.

'Whoever he is,' I stated to my fascinated hosts, 'he used to live in that attic.'

'Pull the other one,' they said. 'Who'd live in that scruffy place? You can barely swing a cat in it. And it hasn't been used for decades.' But I was adamant, so they checked.

Decades ago, there was a mentally sub-normal man living at the farm. The locals were afraid of him but he was harmless. And although he was now 'dead' he still lived there in the attic part where he'd always been in residence. And one of the reporters revealed: 'He was a strange heavy man. He was hugely built too. That's why the children were fearful of him, I think. But the oddest thing about him was his feet. They were *enormous* and he could barely drag them about behind him!' There were raised eyebrows all around after that.

In my years of searching and developing psychic and mediumstic skills I have learned much about the power of thought. I've also experienced, or rather encountered, thought-forms on countless occasions. In Ancient Egypt the Priests of Isis meditated within the dead Pharaoh's tomb creating by the power of their minds 'guardians' or 'thought-forms' to ward off any intruders after the burial. They stood the thought-forms at the sealed entrance to the tombs. This probably gave rise to the so-called 'Curse of the Pharaohs'. But is there any truth in these accounts? I think there is.

When I entered a friend's home I was surprised to clair-voyantly see the figure of a faceless, hooded monk in a black robe standing by the threshold. The form was motionless as I passed it warily, and I said nothing until supper-time. I then described it to my hosts. Robert sniggered. He had read about the guardians placed in the Valley of the Kings and had created his own special hooded monk to test my powers of clairvoyance and see if the theory worked!

These thought-forms, or to give them their more popular name, ghosts, cannot communicate with us in the way that a living, vibrant, real spirit-person can. Ghosts have no conscious personality of their own. Sadly, many mediums have not yet mastered the art of telling the difference between thought-forms and communicators and therefore have fallen into the trap of confusing the two.

A good example of this comes from my earliest days of mediumship before I'd learned the difference myself. I was demonstrating at a Remembrance Day service. As the lights were slowly dimmed in respect for the War dead and the audience fell silent, I clearly saw two servicemen — killed in the Second World War — standing behind a woman. Well, actually they weren't behind her, but sort of hovering at the back of her. I could only see their faces and shoulders. When I described them she replied: 'Oh yes, I've been thinking about them all week.' Glancing back now, I can see that they were thought-forms.

In later times I had quite an unusual experience around the date when the world was horrified and deeply shocked and angered by the Chernobyl Nuclear Reactor Disaster in Russia, where huge amounts of radioactive material was burning and being released upon an unsuspecting world. Britons were told the radiation cloud wouldn't reach the United Kingdom. But while out walking one day I really did feel most unwell. In fact I cut my journey short and called on Sheila, a friend nearby, and asked if I could rest awhile.

'I feel very strange,' I remember saying. 'All my body's tingling and "alive" as though I've been under a sun-lamp for too long.' And I lay down on a bed for half an hour.

On the six o'clock news that night it was publicly announced that the radiation cloud was directly over our area and the radiation levels were 10 times greater than normally acceptable. The price of mediumship is sensitivity I guess.

Critics of mediums are fond of accusing us of constantly reading the minds of sitters, and in fact they claim that most of our evidence given by the spirit-world doesn't come from there at all. This seems to be a rather presumptuous statement. If only *one* case for survival is proven then our claims should carry more weight than this.

I began to search and seek for proof that would baffle even my own sharp intellect; and the spirit-world came up trumps again. As there was no one more sceptical than myself I reasoned that if I could be satisfied, many others would be too. White Owl obviously caught these thoughts, for upon investigation of the messages given out publicly and privately there were always one or two pieces of evidence that were not acceptable at the time and had to be researched. If they proved correct then the theory of telepathy on the part of the medium had to be ruled out. Mediums can't read facts from a mind that does not possess them, can they?

To prove my point I have in my possession a signed affidavit, one of many, which indicates direct spirit-knowledge of details outside the mind of the sitter who received them. Here is the statement signed by Mrs Valerie Johnstone. It speaks for itself.

Stephen O'Brien told me he was talking to my 'two Uncles in spirit, both brothers,' and he named them as 'Uncle John and Uncle George'. I strongly disagreed, telling him I only had one uncle there, namely Uncle John. But Mr O'Brien stuck to his guns.

'There are two uncles,' he said. 'Ask and you'll find I'm right.'

So I did ask my mother, and to my astonishment the facts proved correct. My Uncle George had died before I was born and I had no knowledge of him whatsoever.

This message impressed me because it contained evidence which could not possibly have been read from my mind. How can information which is not present in my memory be gleaned from it?

The only fitting explanation was that my two deceased uncles were speaking to the medium.

13

Poltergeist

My teacher, Mrs Palmer, had taken a sudden heart attack. At the hospital, I took her hand and she smiled, for she knew I was giving her healing. Then we fondly said goodbye, and I left.

As I sat on the bus, Mrs Palmer's guide Ahmed said to me, 'That is the last time you'll see her alive in your world.' And he was right. Before I could make another visit, she passed over.

Her sisters sent me her pure crystal ball they'd found, and gazing into it as an experiment, to my great surprise I could see moving pictures. There was a high-speed train shooting along the tracks; then a Guardsman outside Buckingham Palace — and before I knew it, I was fulfilling her prediction given two years previously. She'd seen me entering London's Spiritualist Association of Great Britain — the largest one of its kind in the world, at 33 Belgrave Square. The SAGB has nurtured within its walls many famous British mediums: Estelle Roberts, Mary Duffy, Helen Duncan, Gordon Higginson, Doris Collins and Doris Stokes, to name but a few. And now I'd joined their ranks.

Working at the Square was refreshing and challenging because their audiences were cosmopolitan. Many people from overseas travel to London just to visit there. This was my first appearance in Britain's capital. And the work was more difficult because I had to pronounce foreign words I'd receive from communicators — some people do have peculiar names!

There were private appointments, groups of sitters and

public demonstrations, and it was bedlam. I'd dash out of a meeting, shoot upstairs in the lift and into another room to take sittings. That kind of pressure wasn't for me, so I decided I'd give a guest demonstration only, whenever I could get to London, in my holidays.

Back home, store work was driving me mad. The hours were long and the pay poor. Then I had an idea. Part-time store work, part-time mediumship — that seemed very sensible to me. I wrote to all the places I served, explaining the position. About 35 letters went out around South Wales, and silence followed.

The days dragged by, and no word came. Why didn't they reply? Was something wrong? Was £2 a meeting too much to ask? And then I received some of the cruellest shocks of my life. Nearly every church slammed its doors in my face. I couldn't believe it. Had they forgotten the years of unstinting service and total dedication I'd given? All those years during which I'd refused to accept service fees and paid my own travelling expenses, even when out of work? Was this really happening? I couldn't believe they were rejecting me with such bitter statements.

I was terribly hurt, because they'd used the medium but didn't care about the man. It was like a nightmare, and their selfishness haunted me for months. Surely they weren't jealous of my success?

Rejected and disillusioned, I took a complete rest. I stopped and took stock of my life and its meaning. I cancelled all my responsibilities and withdrew further engagements. I got right off the Spiritualist roundabout and only kept my part-time job going. And with its meagre wages I barely survived the wilderness months that followed; months filled with heartache and indecision.

I had plenty of time on my hands yet I just couldn't erase the deep wounds those letters inflicted upon my spirit. I wandered round the city shops bleary-eyed, deep in thought and desolation. What could I do now? I was an outcast in my own nation.

I'd been charged with a message of love and hope by a world beyond time and space, but my own people rejected it. And in those days I knew what it was to be a prophet without honour in his own country.

Still lost and dejected,I went up onto a mountain to pray. In silence and all alone I sat on the summit in the midnight mist looking out over distant city lights, twinkling under a black sky speckled with stars. I took in each lamp-lit house beneath me as far as the eye could see. There were lonely people there, sad and grieving people, seekers who needed to hear the voice of the spirit. I could bring that voice. But my soul was broken and all I could do was yearn to be accepted by my own nation. What had happened to my dreams, my desire to touch the souls of people in need? It was slipping away — the purpose of my days had been extinguished.

Gazing out across the dark night, I felt a teardrop hit my hand. And listening to the distant buzz of the city I realized I was learning another of life's hard lessons. Spirituality is rare.

Slowly and painfully, the months tumbled over one another. Winter turned to spring, and it took a long time before I entered a Spiritualist church again. But when I did, a young medium singled me out for a message: 'The sheep have deserted their shepherd,' he said, 'but one day they'll realize that the shepherd was right all along.'

Yet that was small consolation, for the church people held their ground and refused to open their doors. Quite by accident, I learned that groups of churches had been in telephone contact and advised each other not to favour me with public bookings.

In my quiet times, White Owl told me over and again: 'You leave a boy — you return a man; with power and understanding.' He seemed to think they would be in touch, but I didn't really know. But they say that when God shuts the door, somewhere he opens a window. And in my case He did just that.

I first met psychotherapist the Revd John Jewsbury, BA, and his wife Valerie at one of my public meetings, and they invited me to help out at their Thursday clinics where I was called upon to counsel certain patients. The three of us worked well as a team. I attended each week for two years and sometimes gave patients a private sitting if the need was there.

I met manic depressives, obsessional-neurosis cases and schizophrenics. Remembering the case of Sue evokes pathos even now. She was completely out of touch with reality, having bizarre dreams about her dead mother whom she claimed prompted her with bad thoughts of murderous acts. There was very little psychotherapy could accomplish, for poor Sue was psychotic. The spirit-people kept instructing me: 'She'll have to come to a realization that what she believes is not founded on fact but upon fallacy. Once this takes place we can get into close proximity with her mind and help her rebuild reason from there.' But sadly, she's still ill.

One day Mrs Jewsbury got an emergency call for help. 'Will you come with me to see a Mr Kaye?' she asked. 'He says he's possessed by an evil influence and needs urgent help.' I readily agreed, and Val and I set off immediately for a poor area.

We arrived at Mr Kaye's house and knocked on the door. The lace curtains were tweaked apart by a heavy-jowled lady. She was fearful of us I think, for she stepped back. Then a wizened man answered.

'Are you the people?' he asked suspiciously.

'Yes.' And we were ushered inside. Mr Kaye was small, painfully thin and absolutely positive he was possessed by an evil demon. And nothing could shake that conviction.

'It stops me enjoying myself,' he grumbled fearfully, giving precise details of how the 'demon', as he called it, robbed him of any pleasure in his intimate relationship with his wife.

But the 'demon' turned out to be nothing more than a portion of his own personality which he'd supressed for years. When just a lad, his mother never allowed him to be discourteous, use foul language or even think bad thoughts. In short, she'd dominated him and tried to make him as 'pure' as possible in mind and deed. So he reasoned that any bad thoughts or actions couldn't possibly belong to him. They must have originated in someone else — the demon. Mr Kaye was a classic case of a split personality; a schizophrenic. And he refused to listen.

'Mr O'Brien can see into the spirit-world,' said Mrs Jewsbury. 'Have you noticed anyone with Mr Kaye?'

'No,' I said. 'I've searched and there's no one evil there.' But when we took great pains to educate him, he just wouldn't listen. He was still 'possessed'. But the sad truth was that he was *obsessed* by the idea of what his mother considered purity to be. Some parents have a lot to answer for.

As we left we tried our best to prevent him from visiting a 'renowned' exorcist. 'God forbid he should be ridiculed by that completely unnecessary experience,' I confided in Val. But the following week, when we returned as arranged, they'd packed, moved house, and were nowhere to be found . . .

Back in the Revd Jewsbury's private development circle which I led, the spirit-people asked me to sit for physical mediumship, affording them a closer contact with our world; I agreed.

After a few sittings held in a blacked-out room lit only by a dim ruby lamp, I soon fell into a trance state. Sometimes I'd be totally unaware of my surroundings, and at others a blending of minds occurred and I was semi-conscious of what the Other Side said through me. The teachings were usually of a highly educational nature. They had to be. Three sitters had University degrees and the fourth was an undergraduate. But there was still room for fun!

Soon a young lad called Bobby spoke, and rapped on the antique bookcase glass. It sounded just like a stone pelted at a window, and we all jumped out of our skins! We fully expected to find the glass smashed, but there wasn't a mark on it.

After another séance I was to stay the night in their home. But during the session there were three deafening thuds high on the ceiling above me. Bobby again! But I didn't give it another thought until I retired to bed, with nothing on, as usual. Imagine my horror when I laid down on spiky pieces of gravel!

Bobby's ceiling raps had been exactly underneath my bed. What a cheeky lad!

'You'll have me punctured!' I admonished as I heard him giggling. 'If you must bring gifts, bring money!' And he laughed. But the most remarkable phenomenon we obtained was transfiguration. Each week, with the ruby lamp shining on my face, the Other Side would take control and take ectoplasm from us and direct it to my head. Under specific conditions they slowly condensed it into a mist and then communicators moved into this and their features could be seen.

The circle reported many successes. But one night I decided to call it a day after an exceptionally unnerving experience. The misty-skin had formed, as I felt my head tilting right back in my chair until my face was pointing at the ceiling. My eyes were tightly shut. Then in a semi-conscious daze, I heard a man speak through me to the sitters. 'This is silly,' I thought. 'I'm talking to the ceiling and they're replying.'

But after the circle I was utterly stunned when they told me my eyes had been wide open and my head had remained directly facing them *all through as the man spoke*.

'But that's impossible,' I frowned. 'My face was pointed *upwards* and my eyes were *closed*.'

'No, your eyes were *open*,' they countered, 'and what's more they were light blue, not brown!'

I was absolutely shocked. If my eyes had been open, surely I'd have seen the ruby lamp and my friends seated before me? But I didn't. The only explanation was that my spirit-head must have exteriorized, tilted backwards and faced the ceiling, while my physical head stayed facing front. I'd been conscious in my spirit-head, not in my physical!

After that shock, I decided to keep firmly in control of myself, so these sittings were temporarily suspended. But that didn't mean that my work for the Other Side had stopped. Far from it — in fact, it steadily increased and I was called upon to deal with a constant stream of new experiences.

One that springs readily to mind was that of my next-door

neighbour, Willy, who lived with his two sisters. One day our front door crashed open and one of Willy's frightened sisters stood gasping for air in the hallway. 'Please come quickly!' she gushed emotionally. 'It's Willy, he's collapsed blue-faced on the stairs. He's fighting for breath — please hurry and help us!' So my father and I dashed next door and lifted Willy up the stairs and onto his bed. I raised his feet above the level of his waist to aid blood flow, but *I* could see what the others couldn't. Willy's spirit had passed. What we emotionally witnessed was only the last throes of the body's nervous systems fighting valiantly to keep the body alive. But Willy had died.

They sent for a priest immediately, but he was too late. Nevertheless he performed the last rites to ease the anguish of Willy's sisters.

Everyone thought that was the end of Willy's adventures on earth. But all of us — including me — were quite mistaken. The following night, as I sat quietly reading by the fireside, my hackles rose as I sensed a strange presence drawing near. Then I gasped in surprised. It was Willy! He hadn't even been committed yet, but here he was gliding through our living-room wall which joined us to next door. He angrily shouted at me: 'Why can't they hear me in there!? They're ignoring me! What's the game?' So I had to tell a 'dead' man that he had 'died'. I explained it all very gently to him and advised him to call for help to meet some of his people Over There. But he just shrugged off my suggestions, and still rather annoyed he ran off through the wall, presumably to try and make himself heard again.

It was only a few days after this that I saw Willy's brother sitting on a bench near town. And as I passed I had to rub my eyes to see if I was dreaming. There was Willy sitting right beside him! He obviously had no intention of moving on to better things. He was keeping to his normal routines, and no one Over There could alter that of course. So off they both went to the pub together — one in the spirit and the other in the flesh.

I didn't hear from Willy again after that, but I confess I did ask White Owl to keep an eye on him and help in whatever way he could. And I'm sure he reached his relatives safely after his short spell on earth.

As time slipped on, back home Dad and I were passing through our darkest patch yet. We'd never really got on well, but now our relationship was so bad that I'd moved into my bedroom upstairs; when *he* came in, *I* went out. We lived in the same house but we didn't share the same space. I'd tried everything in my power to get a peaceful life, but it was no use. It was a pure personality clash that seemed impossible to resolve. Silently I vowed that before I'd tolerate any further harassment I'd move out and sit on an orange-box in the street if it meant that was the way to be let alone. And someone, somewhere, must have been listening to me, for that's almost exactly what happened.

I'd already received a letter from the Housing Department informing me I was now at the top of their list after two year's wait, which was just as well because while walking home a different way one evening I spotted a furniture van outside some maisonettes. I now know that I was inspired to pass that place, for I immediately applied for the tenancy, and within two days it was granted and I moved in.

I threw my meagre possessions into 13 black plastic bags and some friends helped me to walk to my new home. I think Dad had the idea that I'd be back in a week, but I knew differently.

So there I was, installed in my first home of my own. I sat on the floor against a wall, gazing around bare walls and carpetless floors. Everything would have to be scrubbed and cleaned — there was such a lot of dirt on the floors — the previous tenants obviously weren't as clean and particular as I was. And so my last few pounds went on cleaning-stuffs and materials. Now I was penniless.

I just sat there, wondering why it had all come to this. And then it struck me that my silent wish had all but come true. I had absolutely nothing. No money, no chairs or furniture, no table, not even a stove. I didn't even possess an orange-box to sit on. I had the flat and that was about it.

But despite all this, I felt reasonably happy, for at last I could come and go as I pleased. At long last I had a place of my own and the peace of mind I'd so avidly prayed for. As for the loneliness, well, I'd just have to get used to that in time. But then the strangest things started to happen all around me, and I began to realize that I wasn't alone at all. My flat had another occupant, and he wasn't of this world. I'd moved in with a poltergeist!

On my first night I slept on the floor and lit a few night-light candles for company. But it turned out I didn't need them, because the air buzzed and hummed with psychic activity, making it impossible to sleep. People were peering at me and getting closer and closer. But worse was to come . . .

Lights were flicked on and off, coat-hangers were thrown across the landing, and from an upstairs room came a man's loud coughing and the sound of footsteps walking the floor above. Shortly afterwards this troubled spirit ripped a tapestry from the wall and tried to pull the bedclothes off my bed. I was so nervous at first that I called a friend in to stop with me until the house was cleared. But little did I know it would take three weeks to accomplish this.

It was a long, difficult haul. Just when I thought I'd frightened off the intruder, important papers of mine were discovered scattered all over the living-room floor, as I clearly heard a man's voice saying: 'We'll get him tonight.' Then I suddenly caught sight of the culprit. There he stood as large as life, screeching out that I should leave his property at once. He said his name was Tom and he was the rightful owner. Showing selfish Tom the rent book didn't do much good either. 'Get out of my house!' he screamed, blue in the face. 'Get out or I'll do something I'll regret!' And with that he snarled and disappeared into the store-room where I heard him talk with two other spirit-people.

Once again I'd completely failed to realize that my psychic

powers had given him an energy-boost; new, vibrant psychic strength which enabled him to create havoc around me. And of course, my annoyance must have shot further energy into the atmosphere for him to use. But I was determined he wasn't going to win. This was *my* new home, not his, and he would have to see sense and leave.

White Owl was most helpful, not in removing Tom and the others — I had to do that, but in the advice he gave.

'Ask about the property,' he inspired; 'and this man had a police record when on earth.' These were the two 'clues' that put me on the right tracks to clearing my home. Enquiries revealed that my flat had been a troubled spot. There was once an active prostitute living there, and then a family who kept a horse in the lounge, and then people who were in and out of prison all their lives. Little wonder the psychic atmosphere was disturbed!

When I thought about White Owl's words, I guessed that selfish Tom's involvement with the police would be the chink in his armour, and so I determined to make full use of it — I had to, I'd tried everything else and still he wouldn't budge. So when next he manifested, I threatened him with calling the police and gave him 24 hours to move out or else. I must say I found it hard to make it sound convincing; but it worked! Tom and his companions left my home and were helped to find their rightful place in the spirit-world. And my little flat gradually transformed itself from a psychic nightmare into a haven of peacefulness.

But these first days on my own were extremely difficult. I was now out of work, and had no money. My stomach began to rumble and I lost weight. Even the clothes I wore started to fray and there was nothing new to replace them.

Life was gloomy and days were full of uncertainty and a deep insecurity about making my own way in life. On top of all this, back came that chillingly haunting sensation of 'not belonging in the world'. At times, in my life as a recluse, I was completely swamped by the most utterly devastating sense of total loneliness; not personal, physical loneliness — I had long-since discovered that the most important relationship I would ever have is the one I have with myself. No matter where I go, or what I do, I cannot ever get away from myself, and therefore this relationship comes first (and all others are secondary). No, *this* loneliness was the blackest shroud of universal alone-ness I had ever experienced, as if no other living being anywhere in the cosmos had any idea of my existence. It was as though my mind was expanding, stretching outwards to the very darkest Edge of Time; and with this expansion came the fullest knowledge that I did not belong on earth — my loneliness was caused because I was lost and far away from my true home: the Realms of Spirit.

It was in these sombre hours that I was told by my Other-World companions: 'We cannot promise you *true* happiness in your world — only in ours.' And I fully understood them. Stranded on some tiny speck of cosmic rock and dust, washed by pale blue seas, I was only visiting this planet.

These reflections were then interrupted by the hollow growlings of my empty stomach and the cold bare floors and walls of my shabby flat. I just didn't know how I would manage to survive from day to day. And when I turned out my pockets, they were completely empty — and I didn't know where the next meal was coming from . . .

14
Pastures New

That first Christmas in my new flat the snow never stopped falling. In my bare living-room I sat at the window admiring the crystal rooftops. All the nearby slums had gone and in their place was a glistening-white blanket.

My new neighbour went to the pub across the road every night and old Muriel was determined the ice wouldn't stop her. Although we were snowed in, two men came over and dug a pathway to the door, slipped and slid her over for her usual nightcap, and then carried her home singing 'I did it My Way', as usual.

I went to the cupboard and, like Mother Hubbard's, it was bare. No money, no food, and on top of all this, no decent footwear to brave the elements. It was the worst winter Britain had seen for decades. Thick snow covered cars and obliterated houses and gardens. Transport came to a standstill. Farmlands and villages were cut off from civilization and phone lines fell in the drifts.

And I was crunching through the snow wearing my only pair of shoes which leaked through splits in either foot. I wrapped two plastic bags around my feet to try and prevent ice seeping through. I applied to the government for new footwear but they refused. How hard and bitter red-tape can be when you're genuinely in need. So I suffered in silence. Until one day I exploded at the Social Services staff. In the midst of my shouting, a girl at the back of the queue called out: 'Don't bother, love. If you dropped dead in front of them, they'd ask for your death certificate to prove it.' And an elderly woman said: 'God help, he's a genuine case too.' And everyone clucked in agreement with her.

'Well, you're on your own again, Stephen,' I thought. And I was. So I trudged home to my ice-cold, empty flat again, miserable. I kept saying to people, 'It's never been so bad. I don't have tuppence to call my own.' And I couldn't help weeping when alone.

Then one morning I awoke drowsily from a deep sleep and rubbed my eyes. Was I dreaming? There on my bedside table were two old pennies, both out of circulation. They were gifts from the spirit-world: One English King George V, dated 1920, and one Irish penny dated 1937! I was thrilled with them and kept flipping them over to delight my friends. It was then I was told by an inner voice: 'We took them from an old grave.'

I immediately let them drop. 'You might have told me sooner,' I complained; 'I'd have washed them first!' How much better if they'd brought me £200! But, of course, this was another valuable lesson. I knew what it was to be poor.

I soon realized that as work was scarce I'd have to return to the theatre, rather reluctantly. I got an agent for television walk-on parts. Only we weren't referred to as walk-ons — we were Supporting Artistes, if you please. And it was tough going. I'd be up at 4 a.m. and off in someone's car to the studios for a costume call at 6 a.m. On one assignment we were filmed on a freezing cold mountain-top having to pretend it was summer. But it was the depths of winter with hail lashing down on us! Even though the countryside was lit with huge orange arc-lights creating a warm sunset effect, we Supporting Artistes were perishing cold, all huddled together in the long grass. 'I must be mad,' I thought.

Filming was very sparse work and assignments were so irregular that I had to wait months sometimes between calls. So in my spare time I helped out at a local playgroup. About 15 toddlers attended each day and they were full of beans! It's easy to see why their mothers left them for four hours! They'd scoot around in pedal-cars bumping into my shins and screeching with delight. And as soon as Storytime arrived, I'd be swamped by children clambering up over my back and shoulders!

But this charity work was without payment, and slowly I reconciled myself to being destitute. And White Owl said: 'How can you help those in the greatest need, if you have never experienced these conditions yourself?' Of course, he was right. I had to learn Acceptance, and the Grace that goes with it.

And so I turned to the creative arts, filling hungry hours with recording my thoughts in poetry. And this soul-stirring exercise helped me to understand my life and, most of all, myself, so that when I was down to my last 20 pence I managed to retain my sanity and inner peace.

But then I had to borrow some money, for news came that my grandfather was dying. I immediately travelled to see Grancha. Entering his room, I was shocked to find him just a shadow of the fine man he once was. His cheeks had hollowed out and his eyes had sunk well back into their sockets. It was cancer, and I couldn't help remembering my mother and her passing.

The old man opened his tired eyes as I took his hand. 'Hello, boy,' he said, and a smile lit up his face: he'd recognized me. Then weakly he muttered: 'I've seen them, Stephen. All my family's waiting for me across the river.'

'I know,' I replied softly. 'Grancha, why are you fighting this? Why don't you just lie back and relax?'

His lips half-flickered. He knew what I meant. And just then, the wall behind him faded away and in its place came a sphere of luminous golden light. Within this stood a beautiful young woman in a silver robe, her arms outstretched, her long dark hair cascading over her shoulders — she was the loveliest sight. She brought such purity and radiance. Then, smiling at me, she spoke: 'I'm waiting for him, Stephen. Two days.' And with those words the light faded and the wall was back in its place.

Who was she? Not wanting to disturb Grancha any further I didn't mention her, and placed his hands inside the warm covers. Then I reached over and kissed his forehead. 'Goodnight — God bless,' I said, just as I had done to my mother.

Exactly two days later, Grancha died, as predicted. But weeks after this I heard a woman say to me: 'I'm Myra, I met your grandfather.' And enquiries proved revealing. Myra was his long-lost stillborn daughter. How comforting to know she met him. And I suppose she was also there when my grandmother joined them all a short while afterwards.

By now, Wales had woken up to the fact that I was still alive and mediating! Glowing reports of my meetings started to appear in the press, and suddenly I was overwhelmingly in demand again! I became a 'personality' virtually overnight, and was once again warmly embraced by my own people, no longer outcast. As White Owl had correctly foretold, I had returned as a man 'with Power and Understanding'.

I began travelling and eventually became a nationally-recognized visionary; people started booking small halls for me to demonstrate my mediumship. Then I was invited to teach at Stansted Hall College of Psychic Science in Essex — the magnificent Stately Home of Spiritualism, reverberating with peace and power and top-class mediums. 'I could live here in the manner to which I'm unaccustomed!' I wittily quipped.

But the work was taxing and I knuckled down to private sittings, lecturing, teaching and demonstrating my mediumship to students from all parts of the world.

On the last night of one week, everyone had had such a good course that they all stood and sang the Welsh national anthem in a moving tribute to my work. As the beautiful melody rose and the words 'Land of My Fathers, how fair is Thy Fame' rang out, my eyes filled with tears; I felt so humbled to be honoured in this way. Then at the end of the song everyone applauded loudly.

I had 'arrived' as a recognized medium.

Back home, things were hotting up now and requests started to pour in for meetings and other duties. The very first funeral I took was that of old May. I restlessly turned in bed thinking about the service the following morning. What could I say about her? I'd have to be careful for she was very crotchety in her last days, probably because of the pain. Nevertheless, she had been a difficult person. Then suddenly I heard noisy, aggressive raps behind me in the darkness. Then there was a loud thump on the floor, and within the mattress came a dull explosive thud. Startled, I rapidly turned around and saw old May directly before me. Furrowing her brow and poking me hard in the ribs with her walking stick, she ordered: 'See you get it right! And do it properly!' But she needn't have worried. With White Owl's inspiration the service flowed beautifully. But fancy her bossing me around before her own funeral!

I also named little Charlotte and her young brother; this is the Spiritualist equivalent to a christening. When I handed Charlotte her white flower as a symbol of purity and love, she delighted the gathering by promptly eating it! How we laughed.

Public demand was increasing all the time, and this led to a meeting being organized by 12 dedicated seekers at a pavilion on the seafront. I was closely involved with it and suggested the monies raised be given to two charities, the Friends of the Blind and a local handicapped children's society.

When news got out and the big day arrived, my telephone rang. On the other end was the BBC wanting an interview.

'What, *live*?' I gasped as my heart skipped a beat.

'No, recorded for the six o'clock news tonight.'

So as quick as a flash I was chauffeured 50 miles by the BBC to their studios in Cardiff, where they whisked me down a warren of corridors and into a make-up room — just like a VIP.

'Oh, you're young, aren't you?' chorused the make-up girls, all cramming in to see what a medium looked like. And while I answered a barrage of questions, the attractive newscaster Noreen Bray entered. She seemed slightly taken aback when I looked her in the eye and respectfully suggested I hoped she wasn't going to humiliate me and my work during the inter-

view. That had happend before, and now I was wise. She
pleasantly agreed not to.

In the intensely bright studio I settled down nervously.
Noreen said she'd read an article about the forthcoming
meeting in Wales' national newspaper and then we were
counted down and suddenly silence fell about us; three huge
cameras slid silently around like menacing robots . . .

As I left, the BBC switchboards jammed with callers. But
outside in the car my chaffeur was giggling at my bright orange
face — I'd still got the make-up on. I sallied out, 'Home James,
and don't spare the horses!' and we sped off along the motorway
to get to the meeting on time.

The next thing I knew we were trying to find a parking space
outside the pavilion. It was a sell-out and there was no room.
People were milling about squabbling for seats we didn't have,
and eventually I pushed my way through to the dressing-rooms.

Gordon Higginson and Mary Duffy were pacing about like
caged lions, while I tried to relax quietly. Each medium has
their own way, I guess. Then suddenly the door burst open and
a white-faced organizer cried out, 'It's like a mad-house out
there!' Then she took a huge breath and went bravely back out
into the fray!

The audience sounded like a football crowd before a match.
Worse still I couldn't get a link with the spirit-world — and I
was to go first! I began to get anxious. Had the trip to the
studios exhausted me? I couldn't go on stage without a message
for *someone*. But still not a sight or sound entered my mind.
Then we were called to commence and the door opened and a
wall of excited voices almost bowled me over. The atmosphere
was filled with electric anticipatio . Every seat was filled! A
more than capacity audience stood around the walls, sat on
tables, and there were no aisles left. This was my first big
meeting and over 700 faces were glaring at me as I gingerly took
my seat. There were people all around me, to the left and right,
and some of them touched my coat and called out greetings as
I'd made my way through the crowd. And still I had no contact

in my mind. But as I looked about the hall I wondered if I could ever possibly meet the needs of these folk. What was it they expected of me? So many demands, so many hopes. Could I meet them? The deafening applause ceased gradually, and still no voices reached me. The £500 raised was presented to the charities and the capacity crowd lifted the roof with clapping and cheering. I'd kept my promise and helped people in need, but now I was in need myself. Where were the voices? Why couldn't I hear them?

Then the chairperson said: 'Ladies and Gentlemen, Mr Stephen O'Brien.' I didn't need to get up, the thunderous applause raised me from my seat. I stepped nervously to the microphone . . . and then a voice said, 'We're Gwen's mother and father.' Thank God! At last!

After a few nervous comments, I delivered the link which was instantly accepted and the evidence flowed without fault. After that my confidence burgeoned and my demonstration rolled along fine. One link followed another; husbands reunited with their wives, daughters to mothers, neighbours to friends. It all went beautifully. The Other Side had not let me down. Why did I doubt them? When I resumed my seat, they clapped and cheered and people whistled out from the back of the hall. It was a success!

Later on I watched the video-recording of my earlier news interview that millions had seen. What an horrendous experience!

The following week, with much public acclaim, I opened the Swansea Psychic Centre (with 12 other colleagues), dedicating it to the service of those in need and those seeking greater knowledge. I was the Vice-President of this educational establishment, and for the next three years took workshops, lectures, discussions, and trained mediums to develop their powers to serve mankind. And the audiences grew so large that most times we had to turn people away; so we moved to bigger premises.

The Centre helped many worthy charities through my

meetings, including Save the Children, Mother Teresa of Calcutta's Mission, an Ethiopian famine appeal, local hospitals needing oxygen tents for ailing babies, and Blind societies. We also raised money for a local school for the physically handicapped. 30 children there needed their own hydrotherapy pool. The organizer told us: 'If you could only see the children's faces when the water gives them their freedom, you'd realize why we want our own pool. I now have to choose *one* child from 30 every fortnight to travel 15 miles to the nearest place. Which one would *you* choose?' I couldn't say: they were all beautiful children, but their handicaps were great. Little James looked just seven years old — but he was 16. It was a great privilege to help them.

Then one day we found ourselves at the centre of public attention. Three colleagues and I were called to investigate the Grand Theatre, thought to be visited by dead Victorian Opera star Madame Adelina Patti, who left a smell of violets in her wake.

When we arrived we were stunned to be greeted by BBC and ITV film crews, radio and press reporters — 20 in all — who'd turned up to record us. Millions would see the TV documentary they were making on the paranormal.

The three ladies and I sat hesitatingly on the stage and all at once people with microphones, cameras and lights appeared from nowhere.

'Give us a rehearsal,' they said.

'Sorry,' I replied, 'but it happens spontaneously.' And they glowered at me over their cameras as though I'd insulted them. The power-circle fell silent, and dozens of switches clicked on.

'I could well contact someone belonging to one of you,' I reminded them. 'And if I do, please speak up.' There was no reply. But, undaunted, I began. And I got an immediate link.

'It's a chap who is a musician. He says he can play the harp and sing. And he's worked on these boards.' Then he called out to me: 'Tell them it's Rye ... I'm here!' So I did. My communicator was the famous Welsh comedian, singer, musician and film celebrity, Ryan Davies.

You could have heard a pin drop in the auditorium. This wasn't what they'd come to hear, yet Ryan quipped: 'I'm sorry to interrupt boys, but I'm taking this opportunity to stage my comeback.' Then in typical style and wit he told them, 'I'm dead but I won't lie down.' He then gave personal facts about his passing and his family. He'd died of heart failure in America following a severe asthma attack. He described his last minutes fighting for breath but so tired of these attacks which had plagued him. He named one of his daughters and sent his love to his wife. He also passed on a message to his comedy-team partner Ronnie Williams: 'Tell him all our misunderstandings are forgotten.' And then he said, 'I didn't finish my contract.'

Three people present that night knew him or had worked with him. And Ryan, whom I never met or knew, seemed like a sensitive caring man and I instinctively sensed he wanted the world to know there was a life beyond the grave, and he'd used me to do it.

When we walked out of the theatre, we filed past silent film crews and stunned reporters. The next day I was at Cheltenham when the news broke in the newspapers and on radio. I was sorry about that, because no one had respected my request to first gain permission from Ryan's wife to print the séance details. The only reason I record them here is that Ryan himself used my mediumship to get across a message of hope to countless thousands who might be grieving over lost loved-ones. When all the emotion and publicity died away, the fact remained that another soul had communicated and reached the people with the truth of survival.

The Psychic Centre was booming and its work, as well as my own, had gained national recognition. And yet somewhere in the back of my mind a strange feeling stirred within me. I couldn't fathom it out, but all I knew was that a new stage of my life was about to begin. I kept telling friends that I'd experienced a great deal of unrest. Then I knew I should move away.

It was a sudden realization. I just knew I had to work in pastures new.

So I registered my flat on the exchange lists on 14 August and that same night two friends suddenly declared: 'Let's have a table-tilt!' Without further ado we sat in dimmed light, our fingers lightly touching a wooden table. Immediately the Other Side sprang into action and the table leapt up and began rocking and swaying to and fro with great vigour. And it tapped out a message — a prediction: 'Within 10 months you will move to Newcastle-upon-Tyne, England, to continue your work.' Then all at once, it abruptly stopped. There wasn't another movement, and the séance was over . . .

Time passed, and just before the 10 months was up I said to White Owl: 'You've never been wrong before, but you are this time'. Yet once again the last laugh was on me . . .

That night, the telephone rang. I shouldn't have been in but my lift was late. At the other end of the line was a man's voice: 'I'm on long distance. Do you still want to move to England?' My heart jumped into my throat. The prediction was coming true! The voice came again: 'Hello? Do you want to come to Newcastle?'

'But what made you ring me?' I gabbled. He'd read my details at his Housing Offices, and then came the mind-shattering statement: '*I've only just decided to move.*' But White Owl had known this 10 months previously. Then I looked at the calendar — *13 June*. Just one day within 10 months. White Owl was right.

The next few weeks were hectic and exhausting. Bit by bit my home was being packed away in cardboard boxes. Still poor, I sold some items and rented a three-ton truck, and six friends helped me load my possessions into it. Within two hours there was nothing of my little flat left — just bare walls and hollow, empty rooms. I gazed around it for the last time and found myself whispering, 'Thanks, we've served each other well.' And then I finally closed the door on it and hurried quickly down the stairs and out into the rain, biting my lip.

Three drivers sat in the truck cabin, as I hugged my friends and kissed goodbye to the hills and valleys of Wales. With tears streaming down my face I entered the back of the truck and they closed the doors. It all happened so quickly, I couldn't believe it.

So began the most bizarre journey I have ever made in my life. For the next 10 hours I sat in semi-darkness, coughing and spluttering from exhaust fumes, until 400 miles later I arrived in northern England. Then like Royalty I was slowly lowered by the hydraulic van lift to a burst of applause from my friends, who made me kiss the ground that was to be my new home.

15

Passing Through the Veil

'I'm afraid to die, Stephen,' whispered my dear friend Pat.

'Don't be, Pat,' I said. 'There's another life awaiting you. There's nothing to fear. It's just a crossing, an awakening to a new world.'

I sat with Pat, whose tired body had been ravaged by disease for over two years. Her hair had fallen out, her skin had become pale and drawn, and yet despite it all she'd kept a sparkle in her eyes. My words seemed to comfort her a little. But she was truly set at peace when I described her long-dead mother's presence in the room and told her she was holding out her hands to her and saying: 'I'm offering the hand of friendship.'

'Oh, Stephen,' beamed Pat, 'Mother always used that phrase.' And this knowledge eased her suffering and calmed her anxious mind. Pat's mother promised to meet her at death's gateway, and kept her word when Pat joined her a short while afterwards.

We 'die' every night when we go to sleep. Just as soon as our physical body has relaxed the spirit body within starts to loosen from it. Then we leave our sleeping form and can travel into the spirit-world as we may. Some evenings we may not travel out, and on these occasions the spirit-body exteriorizes from the physical and remains close to it, in a state of semi-sleep. This gives our spirit-part the chance to absorb cosmic energies about it and channel them naturally to the sleeper.

One early morning when I awoke I couldn't move my left arm

at all. It was as heavy as lead and freezing cold. Then I saw a dark shadow of its exact shape and size, floating down and moving into my physical arm's place in the bed. The circulation returned and my 'dead' arm woke up!

Another morning, before I could properly move my body, I only thought about taking a shower and I shot out through the bedroom wall, still horizontal in my spirit-body, and landed in the bathroom! Taken aback, I gasped and then shot back into the bed. That was the quickest shower I'd ever taken!

Once on a bright starry night I was wandering along the cliff tops when I saw a 'sleeper' appear in the air about 30 feet above the calm waters below. He must have wondered what the sea was like and was carried there by his thoughts. I've also seen people I *know* who have appeared to me when they were asleep. But I know they haven't passed over properly because they don't carry a bright light with them, as permanent spirit-visitors do.

Sudden deaths, such as accidents, cause many people to go into a state of concussion. Just as the earthly body is knocked unconscious, so the spirit suffers from a temporary state of sleep. But this soon corrects itself and consciousness returns. But when long and protracted illnesses are involved, the passing is taken more gently and loved-ones in the spirit-world gather to meet the traveller as he crosses the threshold of death to life.

Of course my experience has taught me that every passing is different. But in each case there is no pain involved. Pain belongs to our physical form only, and it isn't present in the finer body.

There are people Over There whose job it is to watch for new arrivals whether they pass suddenly or gradually. These Watchers are especially evident in world disasters such as war or the dropping of atom bombs or large-scale tragedies. And people who are in states of coma are already passing in and out of their physical bodies. As the casket sleeps, the spirit is released into worlds beyond earth. When the Nazarene said

'Lazarus, come forth!' he called back the spirit which was wandering, but the body was *not* dead. If it had been then no reanimation could have taken place.

The same applies to people on life-support systems — I've learned that over the years. If the spirit vacates permanently then the person has 'died' and the body is kept 'alive' only in a mechanical sense. It isn't animated by the spirit but by a machine. Switch off the machine and the body ceases to function because the spirit is gone.

But perhaps the best people to talk about passing over from one state of life into another are the people who have had that experience, and who can speak from first-hand knowledge. Through my mediumship I have several accounts of these, but the following two might interest us most because they are my mother and White Owl. They have dictated their words to me and I've faithfully recorded them. Of course, because their words are passing through my mind they're bound to be coloured by my phraseology. Nevertheless, despite this inevitable happening, their thoughts are still soundly transmitted and their experiences are valid and helpful. As you read them, then, don't fear the Dark Angel called Death . . . for He isn't a Dark Angel at all. He's the Brightest One . . .

Here is my mother's passing as seen from her viewpoint:

You were all gathered around the bed. I don't know if you knew that I could see you all, but I could. My old body was wracked with pain and numbed by morphine to combat the agony of the cancer but my inner body was alive and well. My physical eyes were half shut but my spirit-eyes were wide open. Gradually, as my strength ebbed away, I slowly lost sight of the bedroom. It just faded away like a scene from a film. And superimposed over it was another scene forming. As earth faded out, my new world faded in. I hadn't gone anywhere. I was still lying in the bed, but I was losing sight of you all. I was so worried I'd never see you again. But someone inside my mind said: 'Lie still. Be at peace. All is well.'

Your physical forms became heavy and grey to my vision. A mist appeared around you. Then inside this mist, a light began to shine. As earth faded out, your physical bodies turned into a grey mist and I then saw your spirit-forms; much lighter and brighter.

The bedroom wasn't duplicated in my new world where I'd arrived. Instead I was in a sort of light-coloured room. I heard you crying and watched you go. I was alone in this room. I couldn't move. I suppose if I'd wanted to, I could have. But the newness of it all made me still as the voice had asked.

Then someone — I thought it was one of you boys — came into the room again. I studied the misty, grey form with its light inside it, but I couldn't recognize who it was. Someone must have been watching closely because that voice spoke to me again: 'It is Mary, your best friend,' it said. Then my vision cleared and I could just make out her features. I saw the rosary beads she was running through her fingers and by some kind of miracle I heard her thoughts. They were quick and clear and packed with love for me. And then, I knew I had died. Mary was asking for my soul to rise to God and to be loved and taken care of there. And I remember thinking, 'It's finished now. Please God, no more suffering.'

And my next thought was: 'Please God, take care of my boys. Look after them for me. And Ron, too. Don't let them be alone.' And I thought of the grandchildren and John's wife and all the others I'd loved. Then I wondered where you were, son. And that voice spoke up again saying: 'Stephen's being comforted. Lie still now, close your eyes and relax , Beatrice. Trust and sleep. Close your eyes and sleep.' And I closed my eyes to rest for a few minutes and then I must have lost consciousness, or the person belonging to the voice must have put me to sleep — I'm not sure. Anyway, after that I didn't remember anything until I woke up a while later.

When I opened my eyes, I was in a very pleasant rest room. It was very spacious, with pale lemon walls and french-windows overlooking a garden full of roses and trees. The sun was bright. I think there was an orchard beyond the garden. The colours were beautiful, very bright and pleasant.

The rest room had three other beds in it, but they were empty. But I wasn't alone. A middle-aged nurse came through the french-windows from the garden and said: 'Hello, Mrs

O'Brien. How are you feeling now?'

'Very well, thank you,' I said. 'All my pain's gone. I feel at peace for the first time in months.' She took my hand. And when she did, I felt a wonderful peaceful feeling as though she'd given me energy. I can't explain exactly what I felt. But I now know it was healing energy.

'All your suffering's over now, Mrs O'Brien,' she said as she smiled at me. 'There'll be no more pain or tears. And just as soon as you like you can get up and walk with me in the garden. The roses are gorgeous. Would you like to come?'

I said I would and pulled back the crisp sheets, expecting to have pain when I swung my legs over the bedside — but there wasn't any. And when I stood up with her help, I could stand straight. I wasn't pulled over by my operation scars like I was on earth.

We walked to the window together. But on the way this nurse, whose name was Totty, must have heard my thoughts because she smiled very reassuringly and said: 'You're worried about your family but you needn't be, my dear. They're quite safe and all is well.'

'Have they had the funeral yet?' I asked. 'What time is it? How long have I been here?'

'Now don't fear,' said Totty. 'They haven't had the funeral yet. And there's no time over here as you'll soon learn. So I can't tell you how long you slept. But I don't think it was very long. Look at the gardens now. Aren't they beautiful?'

And she showed me the fresh flowers. And the birds were singing their songs as though the sun had just come up. It was the loveliest view I'd ever seen. Just what I'd imagined heaven to be like. Totty must have heard my thoughts again because I instantly remembered the family, especially Claire and Johnathan, for Totty said: 'They're all well on earth. And just as soon as you're ready we'll go back, shall we?'

'Can you take me back?' I asked eagerly.

'Only on a visit, my dear. And that isn't my work. But shortly someone'll come and go with you to see them all on earth. I promise you.'

And that was how my mother arrived in the Next Life.

Another moving account and a completely different one at that is given by White Owl, my Red Indian Spirit Guardian:

The love I held for my woman, Running Deer, was well known in our tribe. She was lithe and beautiful. Her eyes outshone the brightest stars and her smile welcomed me each time we met. Other men consorted with many women, but I kept only to her. She meant life itself to me and this caused jealousy among the other men of my day. One, whose name was Tomahawk, wanted Running Deer as his own. We had often fought for her love, and each time she expressed it only to me. One day she and I had been bathing by the river near to the waterfall when, unknown to either of us, Tomahawk crept up behind me as I stood gazing across the banks at the woodland view.

As swift as the lightning that travels across the heavens Tomahawk struck me a fatal blow at the base of my skull with his hunting hatchet. I was told these things after I passed from the earth-plane. At the time, I just felt a shuddering crack of numbing sound in my neck. Then blackness overcame me. Before I lost those last seconds of life, I felt my body falling into the river. I heard Running Deer scream and cry out. But the murderer had taken flight on his horse.

I swam to the bank and clambered up, exhausted by the blow, trying to gain my breath once again. I saw Running Deer wade into the current and drag something from the river's grip. She struggled and panted for air as she pulled the heavy object onto the grass nearby. I shouted out to her: 'I'm alright! He's gone now!' But she took no notice.

Still struggling, she didn't even see me running towards her. But as I approached, I saw what she was kneeling by, crying and mourning over. It was my blood-stained body.

I sat on the riverbank, dumbfounded by the thought of my own death. And then a brilliant light flashed across the moving waters. And I saw the radiant form of my great-grandfather floating across the river. He didn't walk, but glided in the light.

His ancient features that I dimly recalled as a boy were just as I'd always remembered them. He spoke to me: 'Take my hands, little one,' he said. 'The river of life has finished with you now. There's nothing you can do here for this woman. She must mourn her loss. But for you, it is gain. A new sun will shine on you now.'

'But you have been long in the spirit-world,' I answered him.

'Yes, and you have now joined me. Come, little one. The memory of White Owl is now a subject for fable and story-telling around the fire of the young ones.'

'But I can't leave Running Deer,' I protested. He gripped my arm, holding me firmly at his side. 'I can't go yet,' I said, and he released his grip. I walked over to her and knelt beside her weeping form. I touched her bronzed skin once more. I kissed her slender neck. But she felt none of these things. And I was distressed. When I called her name, she did not hear my voice. Then I was aware of great-grandfather nearby.

'You cannot do any good here now,' he told me. 'You are a medium who speaks with the spirits of our ancestors. You should know it is not all who possess such a treasured gift.' And deeply vexed, my tears joining those of my beloved woman, I agreed to follow him.

'Do not fear,' he said, 'I'll bring you to see her soon. Just as soon as you understand . . .' And together we floated out across the river and into a great, engulfing light. The power and brilliance of it swamped my vision, obliterating the scene I'd just left, as I watched Running Deer lift my lifeless form onto my horse, Silver Cloud, and gallop away to give the news to our people.

'Do not be afraid,' said great-grandfather. 'The light will heal you. It will soothe your soul, my son. Just breathe it in.' And I did so. And then, it faded away and a new countryside came into view. I questioned my friend.

'We are at the Hunting-Grounds?'

'They are everywhere!' he smiled. 'But in this small part of the Great Spirit's land you and I shall sit and talk awhile. There is much I have to teach you.' And we both sat on the dewy moss and he told me many wondrous things. He spoke of my new life, its ways, and the future that he said lay before me. He introduced me to my brother, Lame Wolf, who passed into spirit before I was born.

'Why does the sun stay high in the mountain sky, grand-father?'

'Because there is no setting of it here, White Owl. Here there is rest for those who seek it, but no darkness of the night. Come now, we have spoken enough, I must take you on a journey.'

'Have we to travel very far?' I asked him.

'No, my son. We are going to the top of the mountain.' And he pointed out the highest peak above us.

'It'll be a good two days walk.'

'No, it will be shorter than the time it takes the lightning to jump the great clouds when the rains come. Give me your hand.' And as I did so, we were standing on the mountain peak.

'But, how . . .?'

'There is much for you to learn. Behold the valleys and the great plains.' And together we could see way into the distance, right out to the far horizon.

'All this is God's Land?'

'This is just a small part of it. See how the hills slope down into the green valley? Look, just there! There is the place where you were brought into Mother Earth. And here just to its side, is the river that watered our people and the land of our forefathers. But now, you are here. All this, as far as the eye can see, is over for you, my son.' And the old man saw my tears fall gently.

'Do not cry for the past. Pray for the future. You shall once again go back to the earth.' My eyes lit up with expectation. Could I dare look forward to being beside Running Deer again? But great-grandfather heard my silent prayer.

'You shall not take up the flesh again, my son. There is a greater task before you. Somewhere in the time yet unborn, you shall stand beside the soul of a man. This man is not of our race or tribe. He will be born far from our peaceful valleys in a time of turmoil and strife, in a land where many people will have forgotten the meaning of loving, giving and caring.'

'How do you know these things, grandfather?'

'It has been revealed to me, White Owl. I see many things with my inward eye which others cannot perceive. Your task is to bring the white man some peace and truth. In time you will see what I have seen. And when the Great Spirit reveals these visions of another world to you, you will feel pity for those races yet unborn. They will have lost their way. They will be needing our simple truths of the spirit to guide them back onto a pathway of peace, a way of caring for one another and Mother Earth.'

'I don't understand,' I said. And great-grandfather took my hands and with the most beautiful smiling eyes I had ever seen he assured me: 'It is written, White Owl. You shall be a messenger. You will see. I have never lied to you.'

Pausing to gather his thoughts, he stretched out a hand and moved it across the vista before us. And with the utmost conviction reaffirmed: 'In a time yet to come, in a place far from these beauteous mountains, you shall play your part. With a man yet unborn, you shall stand. And together you will bring the Truths of the Great Spirit to all who will cease their wanderings and listen.'

16

Behind the Scenes

Over the years I've often been asked what it's like to communicate with the spirit-people and how I deal with the problems arising when messages are being relayed from one level of being to another. The processes are intricate, to say the least, and it requires a great deal of skill to manage a public demonstration or private consultation correctly, especially when several communicators are trying to gain my attention at once which has sometimes happened.

Here is the story as seen by the medium from behind the glare of the lights . . .

I arrive at city halls or theatres and accustom myself to the surroundings, making final arrangements with sound and lighting engineers and then I retire to my dressing-room to change. If letters and greetings cards have arrived I don't open them or have any contact with outside information such as inscriptions on bouquets or gifts. As much as these kindnesses are greatly appreciated, I try to keep my mind free from anything which may colour it prior to the demonstration.

Eventually the doors are opened and the public flood inside; maybe some without having booked seats, hoping for an opportunity to witness the joining of two worlds. From the dressing-room I hear the droning buzz of hundreds of voices and sense the excitement mounting among the people. At this point I remember that many in the hall are desperately awaiting contact with people they have loved and 'lost'. Some have held on tightly to their tickets for months in advance in the prayerful hope of gaining contact with someone special on the Other Side of Life. To them, their ticket is a passport to relief and renewed hope. The needs of these people cannot help but keep mediums very humble. I can't possibly reach them all, and inwardly ask that those I do touch will find strength and reasons for continuing with their lives.

As the seats fill, the noise of talking swells and sounds like a massive swarm of bees circling the building. I try to relax as much as possible. In the silence of my mind I send out thoughts to those who help me, asking that their evidence may be clearly communicated and that they'll bring details that can be understood. I ask to be given the name of the communicator and the recipient in the hall if possible, so that between us the spirit-world and I can establish the correct contact. And then I know the messages, rightly placed, will flow through me.

Sometimes while sitting quietly I may receive a contact or part of a message at this point before I confront the public. A man might appear and ask for a connection to his wife whom he assures me is in the auditorium, or a child might be heard giving a name and a message for its mother. If this happens I usually respond immediately with something like: 'Stay close to me and we'll try to get your message through,' or, 'Stay with me and I'll do my best to help you.'

The clock ticks away and the final minutes before I take the platform rush toward me. My solar-plexus tightens with anticipation; in the early days, until I learned self control and trust, I used to be anxious to the point of worry, but experience has beaten this fear out of my system. Yet slight apprehension still remains because communication, even at its best, is always an experiment. So many processes can go wrong as I'll explain later.

There's a knock at the door and I'm ready to start the meeting. I pause in the wings to gain my composure, very conscious of the great responsibility placed upon my shoulders. Not only will I be representing the spirit-world and the organization I'm serving, but I am also very aware that by the power of the word I can help and sustain and lift lives shattered by grief. Words can encourage and give comfort and also offer solid evidence of survival — if rightly delivered.

The audience falls silent, the meeting commences and I'm introduced and take the platform acknowledging the audience's greeting. My consciousness begins to register the nearness of the spirit-world now. But it's sometimes difficult to block out the public seated before me; those seas of expectant faces, each one telling its own story, many praying for some contact with that Greater World. I step to the microphone, always commencing the meeting with a talk which may prove helpful to the hundreds listening. It may be a message of reassurance, a true story of spirit-return, a comforting experience given in the hope it may help someone to go on with life even though their dearest people are no longer physically with them. I speak because I know full well that with the magnitude of the gathering and the time allotted to work I cannot possibly touch everyone with a spirit contact. When I'm addressing a crowd I'm talking to each individual personally. It's a little something from me to you if you like. Some education, some thought-provoking ideas being inspired by the Other Side.

But the public are now waiting . . . where is the first contact? All anxiety vanishes as a spirit-person gives me information and details of themselves, which may comprise of places, names, dates, or family matters.

The first job is to place the link. The right connection must be made before the evidence can be relayed. If the message goes to the wrong person the whole object of the evening is defeated. Placing links can sometimes be difficult. Even if you get the full name of the communicator and the person they wish to contact, it's not uncommon for several hands to claim the connection. Some raise their hands genuinely believing the information relates to them, but sadly I must report that others driven by grief or greed will claim a contact just to have some kind of help, even if they know it isn't for them.

At this point I become a kind of telephone-operator between two worlds, though vision is also in use as well as sound. When two or even 20 know the information I ask the spirit to give more facts. This is where we really get to work. The next pieces of evidence usually establish the correct recipient and this in itself displays an intelligence at work behind a medium. When you have hundreds of people all about you, you can't possibly select each recipient individually. In some gatherings all the people cannot even be seen. They're so far away and the glare of lights don't help. This is why the spirit-people directly contact me on the platform, although I do frequently see them standing near recipients in the hall.

Once the link is firmly recognized and placed, the communicator acknowledges this with more evidence. Then the messages flow and reach their target.

Most messages are direct and to the point. Sometimes they are simply-worded but on occasions they can be so complicated that only the recipient can unravel them. I've found the communicators bring whatever they can to be recognized and prove their survival. But they may also speak about parts of their lives or mention remote family details about which the sitter may know nothing. When this happens, people are asked to research and check if the details are correct. This can often be the best evidence of survival because the details relayed were obviously not stored in the recipient's mind, which rules out telepathy by the medium — something we are frequently accused of doing. But I've learned that those who don't wish to believe will never accept, even if the evidence is so startling and correct that it takes their breath away.

The messages can only be fully understood by those receiving them and those sending them. What may sound 'trivial' to the witnesses can convey a great depth and wealth of meaning to the receiver. For example, the link might contain 'code-words' or even special personal references known only to the two people involved. Who can say?

However, I do smile when the spirit-people get their transmissions mixed up. The Other Side inhabitants are just as fickle and human as ourselves and they certainly can and do make mistakes. Just because we die, we don't change immediately and are still very fallible. Once I recall a spirit aunt contacting her niece and telling her she was 'with child'. The delighted young woman confirmed she'd just found out herself. The aunt brought before my eyes a pair of blue baby gloves. She stated quite clearly her niece would have a healthy baby boy. Everyone was pleased with that. But months later, she approached me having given birth to a girl and asked, 'What does it mean?' I said, 'It means your aunt was quite wrong.' She'd probably felt a 'hunch' as many women do and voiced it as a fact. I think we all learned a lesson from that.

I maintain survival is best proven by relating past events and present circumstances mainly — the future is not really the job of a public medium. Accurate prediction is possible of course, and I have been used to deliver it on several occasions.

In all my years of public mediumship I've never had to sit down because I had nothing more to give. In fact, had more time been available I'm sure dozens more spirit-people would have communicated at each meeting. From the very first time I appeared in public the services have flowed, but that's not to say I have never been in difficulty, because I have.

A breakdown in communications is probably the medium's fault, I believe. After all, we are 'tuning-in' to higher frequencies of the mind and that isn't easy. Mediums are rather like human radio sets, but whereas radio-tuning is more or less fixed, the medium's mind is trying to register constantly fluctuating spirit-wavelengths. This registration is carried out by the mind, under strict discipline of the willpower.

Sometimes I catch everything that is given by my communicators but sometimes I might miss small pieces of the message. Some spirit-people can play a part in a communications breakdown too. They forget or get flustered and give the wrong information; just as we would at such an important time. Add to this the poor recipient who has been singled out and now has to acknowledge facts before hundreds and you can quickly see that nerves can prevent people from recalling even powerful emotional memories brought by spirit loved-ones.

It is very rare for a spirit message to go completely unaccepted, but this of course has happened. There are many valid explanations as to why some communications are unclaimed and often the fault lies with audience members being reticent to speak up. They may feel embarrassed about people recognizing their voice when they just wanted to sit unnoticed and simply witness the proceedings. A few may have groundless fears of family skeletons coming out of the cupboard. No medium can have control over any of these natural hindrances which can, and often have, prevented successful communication taking place. Speaking for myself, I never consciously allow communicators to humiliate or embarrass recipients through my mediumship. I can and often do tone down or even reject what is transmitted, for I feel we should remember that death doesn't instantly change those who experience it and I don't think the public platform is the right place for serious family feuds to be aired.

A good example of an unaccepted message which was subsequently confirmed was that of Mrs Gaynor. She wasn't present at the meeting when it was relayed but her friend was and, although she recognized it, for some reason she didn't claim the connection. Apparently I announced to the audience: 'There is a message for a lady who is holding an appointment card for next week at Singleton Hospital.' There was no response so I'm told I continued with: 'Someone here understands this but isn't acknowledging it; nevertheless I'll give the link. Harry says he'll go with you to the hospital and the tests results will show perfectly clear. There's absolutely nothing to fear, you are healthy.' Over a year later, Mrs Gaynor introduced herself to me at a charity shop and related her story, adding: 'Harry was my husband on the Other Side. I was booked to go to the hospital and quite fearful, but that message helped me greatly. The tests were clear just as Harry had told you.' Thankfully

Mrs Gaynor's friend had passed on the information which brought hope and reassurance to a bereaved widow. Though I was pleased that Harry had eventually reached his wife, by not vocally accepting the link when it was transmitted Mrs Gaynor's friend didn't help the meeting: had she spoken up Harry might have given more. I'm quite certain other 'unplaced' links may have also found their targets in time.

I have learned to trust and depend upon the voice of the spirit. I've also learned to flow with the stream of evidence reaching me and not battle upstream by arguing over minor details which seem important to the recipient and mean very little to the spirit-people.

When I work, I'm engrossed and can lose all sense of my surroundings. Once while delivering clairvoyance a lady seated no more than eight feet away from me was taken ill with an angina attack and was escorted from the hall with quite a fuss made, but I was totally unaware of what had happened. This demonstrates that when a medium is working properly a shift of awareness is operating. The contacts flow to me and I'm happy to deliver them for as long as time permits. As the night draws to a close the audience has sometimes been upset because the communications will cease. There are often sighs of disappointment when I'm pulled to time, and people have even called out for more. Once a lady yelled emotionally: 'Please don't finish!' This kind of remark makes me aware of the very unique service mediums can give and the great need there is for it.

As I break my connection with the spirit-world their nearness fades from my consciousness and I once more become attuned to my worldly surroundings. It's not uncommon for me to wonder where I am at such times.

Usually meetings have a question-and-answer session included and these are always interesting and sometimes positively absorbing.

I thank the public for their kind attention, expressing the hope that I may have in some small way helped them or stimulated their thinking. As I bid the audience goodnight there is applause, and on occasions they have stamped and cheered. But, however embarrassing the noise, I'm grateful for I know it's their way of saying 'thank you'.

Communication is never easy. Mediumship has to be developed over a period of years. It has to be channelled correctly and watched carefully like a growing plant or delicate child. It has to be fed time and patience, and if it is undertaken, then it should be done so in a serious and responsible manner. To dabble with anything is unwise; to master anything is always fruitful.

Each day I used to sit in quietness and speak with my spirit-friends to strengthen our links and gain from them any help they might give for my life and work. Being in touch with the Worlds of Light brings great joy and happiness. Sometimes my mother or other family members greet me in my quiet times. While attuned I speak freely about any matters I choose and can receive wise advice if the conditions for contact are right. I may be asked to read certain books to build my knowledge. I obey. Once I travelled 300 miles to get them because they were out of print. At other times I was asked to write guidance for local mediums and others requiring help. I was thanked with: 'Post it off. Sorry we can't supply the stamp!' In this way many people's prayers were answered.

My voices gave me plenty of work to do, and it kept ever in my mind that the task of a true spiritual medium is *to serve*.

Towards the end of a meditation I would sometimes be asked to rest my head back on the chair and receive spirit healing energies. I never refused. I'd soon relax and feel exceptionally light-headed as the spirit power gathered around me . . . I'd wake up fresh and alert a while later.

After one exhausting day's work I felt like a lead weight and slumped into a two-seater settee. I closed my eyes for a second and I heard a loud crack in my mind. My head quickly dropped to my chest, but before it touched my breastbone my spirit-body was lifted out of my physical form by two pairs of hands. How light and wonderful that feeling was. The perfect calmness was marvellous. I still had my spirit-eyes shut tightly while I was gently placed at the other end of the settee. A lady's hands took mine and affectionately smoothed my palms. I realized this was Mrs Palmer, repeating the gesture I'd done to her when I visited her at hospital and gave her spiritual healing not long before her passing to the spirit-world. Then somehow I disappeared into oblivion and awoke half-an-hour later in my physical body back at the other end of the settee! This occurred at a time when my workload was prolific and stress was high, and it proves the adage that 'Those who serve are served'.

Other private communication times occurred at night when the Other Side made itself known as I lay quietly in my bed, just before sleep folded me into restfulness. I'd crash into bed extremely tired and then feel the room 'shiver' — a feeling rather like a water-ripple in the atmosphere. This meant someone had suddenly 'arrived'. They'd announce themselves and then I'd see various coloured spirit-lights floating about the bedroom. In the darkness my friends would then give a healing treatment. I'd feel their spirit-hands smoothing my skin and would receive a little prod when they'd finished. That would be about all I'd remember until the sun greeted me at dawn and the noisy seagulls outside cried their screes and gracks as they fought over titbits placed out for them the previous night.

One night I received a special private link. I was shaken from a deep sleep by hands. When I turned around I was shocked to see a figure watching over me as I lay in the bed. A spirit had fully materialized and was standing there as solid as any human being. In the orange glow of the street lamps filtering through the window I saw her spirit-robes draped over one shoulder and up around her head, leaving a smiling face perfectly visible. I was terrified by the suddenness of the shock — it was like discovering a burglar in the room, an uninvited guest. The fact that she stood there, real and substantial in her flesh-and-blood body with two arms outstretched in love made no difference, I'm afraid. I was just 20 years old and caught unawares. I dived under the sheets and remember thinking speedily: 'If you love me please go away.' And, of course, she did.

I believe the messages that mediums receive are prepared in the spirit-world before they're transmitted. An example of this was when a lady at Stansted Hall College of Psychic Studies came for a private consultation during a week of lectures there. Her grandfather communicated giving his name and began speaking to her for about two minutes. Then the communications completely stopped.

'I'm very sorry,' I said apologetically, 'but I don't receive anything more for you, except there seems to be a confusion here in the spirit-world.' All I could get was the name 'Hutchinson'.

The sitting was terminated and we agreed to try again the next day to see if our luck had changed. It had. This time she was pleased with the results. Then she offered information which clarified the previous day's failure. The sitting she'd attended the previous morning was booked for her father, Mr Hutchinson, but at the last minute *she* had decided to take it instead. The spirit-people were obviously taken by surprise!

Mediumship by its very nature is fluid. It fluctuates in its operation, as indeed we humans do. That's why I always advise people to make a lengthy investigation before making a final judgement upon the evidence. I maintain that the conviction that life goes on after death only comes gradually as piece after piece of evidence is delivered maybe over months or years, rather as though each fragment was a brick in a rising wall. After a while the wall becomes so high, so overpowering in its immensity, that the seeker can then say with certainty that man *does* live after he dies.

But what exactly constitutes evidence of survival? I think evidence means different things to different people. I don't believe that what the critics say they want from the spirit-world would entirely satisfy them. They ask for full names, telephone numbers, dates of death, and other 'precise' information. To a degree, I'm sure this kind of accuracy is necessary, particularly in public meetings where many and varied minds have gathered for an experience, but I do firmly believe that it is the seemingly trivial, intimate memories, phrases and personal instances which can often be most convincing to the average seeker. As I have said before, we should remember the evidence is prepared for the benefit of the sitter, not for the approval of media-men, reporters, or even the witnesses.

I think there will always be those who are unready to accept the fact of an afterlife. There will always be people who will remain seemingly untouched by a display of spirit power. I say seemingly, for who knows what really goes on inside another human being's mind? The hardened sceptic who refutes the fact of another existence beyond death and leaves a demonstration with nothing but scorn for mediumship may be the person holding the greatest fear of dying. One day, even if on their death-bed, they may dimly remember their visit to a demonstration — perhaps this thought may ease their passing and give comfort in their hour of need. I don't believe anything is wasted.

One such shrewd businessman attended a meeting but didn't receive a personal contact. Afterwards he confronted me: 'Without doubt you can hold an audience's attention and present your case well, but nothing you said tonight convinced me there was a life after death.' Perhaps he had overlooked the weeping man seated in front of him who'd received so much detail from his recently deceased wife that his tears of joy couldn't be contained.

'*But I'm not out to convince you of an afterlife,*' I replied. 'I'm here to serve the spirit-world, to link wife with husband, mother to son, father to daughter, so that shattered lives may be pieced together and people can obtain new hope and peace within themselves to face the future.'

His brow darkened and furrowed. I continued: 'When a medical specialist heals the sick, does he do it to prove that medicine works? Or does he do it to serve and aid the suffering?' There was no reply.

Sensation-seeking individuals have asked me several times if I have delivered clairvoyance to the rich and famous or people holding high offices; some are convinced I have given consultations to Royalty. When pressed for details my answer is always the same: 'A private consultation is exactly that — private.' It doesn't matter to me if a king or a pauper comes seeking help from the spirit-people; I'm not impressed by worldly rank. Whether the sitter is a rich man, poor man, beggar-man or thief, to me they are all souls on the pathway of life, meeting its rigours and challenges as best they can. I've found that irrespective of the 'name' or rank they may think they hold, we are just people, all motivated by the same basic emotions and holding the same basic concerns. This world of ours makes much of pomp and ceremony and treasures public acclaim as a mark of importance. But in that Greater Life what we call ourselves or what we think we are is of little account. It is what we *really* are, what we have done with our lives which matters. These are the only eternal treasures we can possess.

Although mediumship comforts the bereaved, heals the infirm, and has given new hope and meaning to countless millions of people, I believe there is a greater purpose behind its function. These comforting aspects are, in my view, a means to an end and not the goal itself. It was summed up to me by White Owl, who wrote through my hand:

> It is our function to touch the soul of man and make him think, helping him become aware that he is a mind, evolving through experience. We desire to make people aware of the infinite possibilities and potential within them, so that they will turn away from the false worship of materialism which creates bitterness, greed and cruelty. It is our hope that people will learn the value of peace and love and project these out into the troubled earth so that the children yet unborn may find a better world in which to learn their experiences when their time for birth is ripe. If we can lift one soul, help one person towards the light of patience, tolerance and genuine caring for its fellow creatures, including the animal kingdoms, then our task has been worth while. For these reasons, and many more, we return to your dark earth bringing with us our light of understanding

which will sweep away all creeds and dogmas and false divisions between nations and replace them with the knowledge that all life is linked and is One under the Guiding Influence of the Great Spirit — the Giver of All. For the God-Force is within everything, behind everything and through everything. When man learns these truths and lives them in his life with the respect for creation that these truths bring, then peace will be his.

And for me, these words ring true. All we shall take with us through the gateway called 'death' is ourselves. There are no pockets in shrouds, no status symbols or earthly aggrandizement on the Other Side. We shall simply take our mind and character, our soul-growth and moral attitudes and all facets of the true inner person. Over There, we shall not be the person we think we are, or the person the world thinks we are — we shall be the person we truly are.

Seek Thyself

Seek Thyself; search not for any other prize,
But quest to find the *Real You*, rather than devise
A plan which leads your search astray:
　　　Glittering baubels all break and die,
　　　And worldly pleasures perish away
　　　(Toys of one life only)
But your spirit stands for always
And you hold the only key.

　　　Lustrous jewels and paper-wealth
　　　Are just for a moment loaned,
　　　And nothing in this world of clay can ever match
　　　The pricelessness of your timeless soul.

A Life Neverending awaits each one at death,
And through the Gateway all must pass:
　　　None can escape,

None can linger at the last breath, but
All must enter the Land where Thought is King;
    An adventure through the looking-glass, wherein
    We will only possess our Total Selves,
    No more, no less;
When we reach Home at last.

So Seek Thyself, O Thee of flesh and bone;
And rest not till the task is done:
    For once You are found
    You can never feel lost;
And when at last Great Peace is yours
You cannot count the cost.

17

Questions and Answers

A much-welcomed feature of my large public meetings is the question-and-answer session that is nearly always included in the evening. Over the years, questioners have posed some deeply searching and meaningful questions in regard to life and its purpose, the paranormal, mediumship, God the Life Force, and other fascinating topics such as Out-of-Body Experiences and the like. I usually explain that I don't know all the answers and whatever help I can give is drawn from my personal experience and the level of understanding I've reached in my quest for truth and knowledge. I would issue the same reminder now.

Here are a selection of questions; hopefully they will be helpful, comforting, meaningful or educational. I cannot possibly include every topic that has arisen over the years, but maybe some of the following will prove stimulating:

Do we all survive death?
Yes. Survival of the consciousness after death is the natural birthright of all.
Even animals and domestic pets?
Yes, indeed. Many of our fellow creatures have returned through mediumship and proved this.
I'd like to ask if you have to believe in a 'God' or any specific religion in order to survive?
No. As far as my understanding goes, we are all a part of the

Life-Force, or Great Consciousness, and it is this which links us to eternal life. All people, all forms of being have this Spirit of Life within them and therefore all will survive death. It isn't necessary to believe this, or follow a particular faith. But if I might say here, what really does matter is *how* we live our lives on earth. When we pass over, we shall gravitate to a sphere of existence which we have earned for ourselves by the building of our character and the growth of our spirit.

So there is more than one spirit-world?

Oh, yes. I understand that there are worlds, within worlds, within worlds, within worlds. 'In my Father's House there are many Mansions', many spheres of existence.

Who selects the sphere we will live in?

We do. The selection is automatic. This may sound difficult to comprehend, but if you can follow my explanation maybe it will help.

It's all a matter of soul-growth. Every kind deed, every truly compassionate thought or noble act increases the stature of the soul — the inner person. The spirit within is growing to be tolerant, more patient, more loving. All these character developments increase the frequency, or rate of vibration, of the spirit-body.

When we pass over, this individual 'frequency' or 'wavelength' becomes naturally attuned to the sphere of spirit-life where it belongs. There are sayings which might help to explain it more clearly: 'Like attracts like', or 'Birds of a feather, flock together'.

So all the evil people have their place and the good have their own spheres?

Broadly speaking, yes — but I'm not happy about that word 'evil'. 'Misguided' is a better term, I think.

If what you said is right, are you telling us we don't change when we die?

Yes. We are the same person one second after death as we were one second before it. Death does not confer upon us abilities and qualities of mind and character which we have not earned for ourselves in this life. However, change is open to everyone. We can always change for the better if we wish to. There's always another opportunity to progress.

May I ask you, do aborted babies survive?

To my knowledge, yes. And they grow to maturity Over There just as they would have done here.

When does life begin?

People are divided on this issue, but I believe that the two life-forms from the male and female involved in the creating of a child are both already alive. The seed and the egg have movement and a certain degree of consciousness. Therefore I would maintain that from the moment of conception, life has begun.

But some specialists don't agree with you. They say the child is not alive, as we know it, until it's served its full term and then taken its first breath.

That is another theory. Even with all our current medical and scientific knowledge, however, we cannot be a hundred per cent certain. That is why I would always give the child the benefit of the doubt.

But should babies be aborted?

I can't answer that. It seems to me that the mother carrying the child is responsible for the final decision in normal circumstances. I believe in personal responsibility.

What do you mean by 'personal responsibility?'

That we are personally responsible for what we say, think and do, and that no one in this world or the next can take away from us the mistakes we have made. We shall have to rectify them eventually and hopefully learn from the growth-experience of facing challenges and meeting them. That is how I see it.

It doesn't seem fair to me that very wicked people can get away with the most heinous travesties of human rights. Why doesn't God stop them?

Firstly, perhaps we should think more deeply and ask ourselves: 'Do they really get away with it?' By committing these acts they have degraded their own souls and thereby 'lowered' their spirit-body's frequency-rate. Nothing we can do can alter this and they will have their reward. One day realization of what they have done and the misery their influence has caused to many people will become clear to them. Then they may reach a time when they feel remorse, and the need to put right what they have wronged. We are our own judges and juries, you see. There is no celestial panel awaiting us when we pass over. We shall confront ourselves with the memories of our acts — good or bad — and pay the price that our conscience dictates.

How is the act repaid?

Usually be seeking forgiveness from the one we wronged, and then by an inner urge to serve them and others, until we ourselves feel that the records have been put straight and we can once again live with ourselves in peace.

As to why God doesn't stop these people committing these acts, I believe we have free will, freedom of choice, the right to govern our lives as we see fit. And this knowledge, of course, brings with it personal responsibility for our thoughts and actions. But our free will is limited. For example, we cannot drink the oceans dry in one gulp, even if we wanted to. There are eternal natural laws at work all the time — restrictions if you like, curtailing our freedom.

I think that these laws, which you can find in all areas of being — emotional, physical, mental and spiritual — are manifestations of what some people call 'God'. I prefer the terms 'Life-Force', or 'Great Spirit', 'Consciousness Itself'; some call this God 'the Law-Giver'. The power of life, and to choose, is ours. God has given us these abilities and it is up to us how we exercise them. We can create beauty and joy, or wreak havoc and destruction. It's up to us — there is not a personal human-being-type God who will interfere.

Why are some people born with such terrible physical and mental handicaps? It doesn't seem fair.

Oh, this is such a hard question to even comment upon, let alone answer. I really don't know if these handicaps can ever be truly justified, which is why I've tried to help people suffering in this way.

My mind tells me that behind everything there is a reason or a purpose operating. I don't profess to know what all those reasons are, but for a moment please could you allow me to give a purely objective viewpoint of this complex problem? A viewpoint which is unclouded by emotion or personal involvement: handicapped people — and we are all handicapped in some way or other — are assumed to have a poor quality of life. Yet that is only our assumption. They may be reasonably happy. If the handicap is particularly severe, the sufferer will need to dig deep down in the soul to find the courage to bear the burden. This is never an easy task for anyone. But by meeting the challenge and hopefully mastering it, soul-growth is achieved.

There is also a theory that these challenges may be necessary for the individual to experience, so that the inner spirit can express some of its hidden beauty. There's yet another theory that man's soul has a debt to pay, a lesson to learn, springing from wrong-doing in a previous life. These are all theories, none of which I would publicly claim as being my own viewpoint. They are easy to trot out, unless you are the one in the wheelchair.

I think physical deformities and mental problems are probably more easily explained by faults in genetic make-up at the early stages of life. But I am not the all-knowing God, please remember.

However, handicapped people seem to me to have some kind of light in their eyes, some kind of special quality which many so-called 'normal' people lack. Add to this a different perception now. From the eternal standpoint, this earth-life is just an eye-blink in the stream of never-ending time. Therefore any earthly suffering is transient . . . it will pass away.

There is no physical handicap in the spirit-body. We are told it functions in perfect health. Certainly the immense courage and fortitude and also the great cheerfulness shown by many handicapped people is a fine lesson for us all. We can learn much from the strength they exhibit.

I don't know if these thoughts help at all, but I did say at the beginning that I do not know all the answers. In fact, I would issue a warning, beware those who profess to do so.

God is perfect, so why did he allow Thalidomide babies to be born with no limbs?

There are two sections to that question. First of all, how do we know that God is perfect? God may be slowly evolving, just as we are; and imperfect beings make mistakes. I'm not suggesting that the Thalidomide case is a mistake by God, I'm just putting forward some original thoughts for consideration.

Secondly, the drug Thalidomide was created by research chemists and released upon an unsuspecting world before adequate testings had been completed. Mothers took this drug in good faith and, sadly, we know the results.

Are you saying God allowed this disaster of modern science to take place?

No, I am saying that God's Spirit is in us all, and certain pieces of that Spirit — the scientists involved — exercised their free will in developing and dispensing the drug, and then mothers took the decision to take it in good faith.

You have said the spirit-body is healthy. What about people who have lost limbs? Will they be replaced on the Other Side?

In our world, if you damage your body or lose a limb, it is only the physical body which suffers. Your spirit-limbs, so the communicators from that world tell us, are undamaged. In fact, cases have been reported where people in hospitals here have undergone surgery to remove a leg, for example, and afterwards they have walked perfectly normally on the missing limb for a few steps, and then realized the true situation. I think it might have been the spirit-leg that supported them.

Will there be a nuclear war?

I sincerely hope not, but it is not my finger on the button.

Is there anything we can do to prevent it?

Yes, create harmony and peace. I think the more people know

about the horrendous effects a nuclear war will have, and the untold misery it will bring, the more governments may realize that in a full-scale nuclear war, there can be no victors.

I don't like the idea of living forever. Who says life is eternal?
Many of those who live in the next world have given that viewpoint.

It would be so boring!
Maybe. Although, what is time? We judge it by the ceaseless ticking of the clock, the rolling seasons, the rising and setting of the sun. But in the next stages of life, there seems to be one never-ending day. The sun doesn't set, therefore clock-time is irrelevant. How then can anyone living Over There gauge time?

You can spend five minutes being absolutely bored out of your mind and it seems like forever to you. Every second drags along. And at other times, you can spend a whole day with good friends and it seems to shoot by in what seems like five minutes.

So what is time? It is an illusion, as we measure it. I think it is all a question of individual perception. I have written many poems discussing such mind-topics.

A medium told me my problems would be solved by my relatives in the Beyond. What do you think of that?
Not very much, I'm afraid. A great part of earth-life is devoted to challenges which we face and overcome; and in the overcoming we may grow in spiritual stature. Our problems are our own. They don't belong to the people on the Other Side, and therefore the solving of them is our responsibility. Besides the obvious facts, I very much doubt whether the spirit-people have the power to interfere with our world to such a great extent.

My niece is on a life-support system, and is 'clinically dead'. Who has the right to make the decision to switch off a life-support system?
This is a difficult question. Firstly we need to remember that we can all exercise free will, and therefore we all have 'the right' to make decisions.

In this case, however, I believe the medical profession place the responsibility of the decision upon the shoulders of the next of kin. This is the universally accepted practice at present. However, as I always say, I do believe that we are responsible for our actions, and whoever makes the decision will have to clear their conscience and be perfectly sure — at least, as sure as anyone can be — that they think the right choice has been made.

Does it matter if a child dies without being 'christened'?

No. All who pass over, old or young, will inherit eternal life whether they have been linked to any set of religious teachings or not.

If a woman marries twice, like I have done, which husband will she live with in the next life?

The marriage pact is a man-made institution; it is of the earth and all earthly things eventually pass away. Legal papers carry very little weight in the Beyond! The woman can live with whom she pleases Over There — it is her choice entirely, exactly as it it is here.

If a couple divorce and one partner still loves the other, will they meet up in the next world?

Again, that is entirely up to the individuals involved. True love will always seek its own.

Do the spirit-people know everything?

Most certainly not. They are only people just like us. The older minds in the Beyond will probably have more knowledge than the younger ones, I think.

Is 'mercy-killing' — euthenasia — right or wrong?

I don't think in terms of rights or wrongs. Decisions are made according to our levels of understanding. What is right to one man may be obviously wrong to another. The acid test is the *motive* for performing our actions. When all is said and done, we have to live with ourselves and answer to our consciences for the acts we commit.

Is everyone met when they die?

I would say yes, but not necessarily immediately, or by the people you might think would be there to greet you. But no one is forgotten in the scheme of things. There are watchers who know when a soul is passing. In cases of illness, as the family on earth gathers, so does the family in spirit.

Why are some houses 'haunted'?
The spirit-people are everywhere! Their worlds interpenetrate ours, therefore every dwelling is 'haunted' so to speak. In homes where you find individuals who possess sensitivity to finer vibrations of energy, you will probably hear of a spirit-person being sighted. However, 'ghosts' are *not* the same as spirit-people. Very often they are energy-pictures held by the psychic fields of activity surrounding the very walls and atmosphere of the building.

What then, is the difference between a ghost and a spirit-person?
A living spirit-person can communicate with you; a ghost cannot. The spirit-person has a personality and is not afraid to express it, especially if you engage them in conversation of an interesting nature. You can talk to a ghost, or energy-picture, until Kingdom come, but you won't get an answer.

Can the spirit-people see our future?
The more evolved souls in the afterlife may have developed this ability, but I don't think many ordinary folk we have loved and known may be able to foresee events — not unless they've developed that special kind of perception.

Should we believe all that mediums tell us?
No. I would say, test everyone and everything with your powers of reasoning and intelligence. Whether you receive 'teachings' or 'truths' from this world or the next, test them all; think them out for yourself and dissect every word until you believe you have discovered their validity or otherwise, irrespective of who speaks these 'truths' to you. People holding a great name do not automatically possess wisdom because of it.

Do you believe scientists should conduct experiments on animals?
No, because animals are not asked to give their consent first. Man experiments on animals because he foolishly deems himself higher in importance than our fellow creatures. I think man would do well to remember that he is also an animal.

I take it you do not eat meat?

That's correct; I'm a vegan and touch no animal produce.

I'd like to know your view on this: is it wrong to commit suicide?

Actions are only right or wrong when each person weighs them against their own understanding and inner code of morals. There are a few factors to consider in the case of suicide victims. Firstly, the action does not extinguish life, it merely terminates it here and places the person in another world. In the majority of cases I understand that people who commit suicide do so because they cannot cope with their lives and circumstances of living. If we cannot cope with life here, it is unlikely that we shall be able to cope with life Over There, for we shall take this 'inability to cope' with us into our new environment. Nevertheless, suicide victims are helped to understand that progress is always available. There are compassionate, qualified specialists in our world and in the next who would be happy to help people try and find a balance in living.

I have heard that if a person commits suicide, they will be in a darkness, a gulf, in the next world, where they must stay until their 'appointed time of death' should have occurred on earth. Then they'll pass into the spirit-world. What are your opinions on this?

I don't accept it. Suicide victims have returned through my mediumship shortly after their 'deaths'. When life terminates here, it continues Over There. That is the law as I see it and have experienced it. I would most strongly not advise anyone to take their own life, however, because I believe that the idea of life is growth. Growth cannot come only in the sunlight, it probably will occur better in the shade. All life is comparison. We must know tears and joy, happiness and sadness, pain and peace within. Taking your life solves no problems — you are still existing. I think it better to learn to cope with your life; seek help if you must, but learn to cope and grow from your struggles and hardships. Surely, it's not what happens to us that matters most but how we *deal* with it that counts?

Are our lives planned out?

If they are — and this is a debatable point — then I believe *we* are the planners. It has to be that way because we have personal responsibility.

Do you think the death penalty should be given to people who commit murderous acts?

It seems to me that we have a problem here. By taking life, all you do is send a vengeful soul into another world; you will be giving someone else your problem instead of having solved it yourself. Capital punishment does not seem to treat the root cause of the issue, which would be to help the criminal redress his character.

Do we have bodies in the Other World?

Of course we do! The spirit is the true person, not the physical body. This earthly form exists because it is built around the blueprint of the spirit-body. Take the spirit away, as in death, and the physical flesh decays because it has lost its animating force.

When we discard the physical, we shall register through a finer vehicle of expression — the spirit-body. It is the counterpart of our present body, and in its own world it is solid and real. It can be touched, sensed and occupies space and dimension.

Can you tell me what happens at death?

Yes, the physical body ceases to function and the spirit-body, which is now the vehicle for the individual to express himself, moves away from the earthly casket. Separation occurs, and once that has taken place the physical body has played its part and will begin to break down into the elements from which it came. The individual will become aware of a different environment, another phase of life.

Is death painful?

No. Disease of the physical body is painful, but death is painless. It is simply the release of the spirit from the earthly body. I often think of it as a happy release, for in many cases it is.

Some mediums charge for their services. I think this is wrong. Do you think people who charge money for their mediumship services

are taking advantage of the bereaved and the vulnerable?
Mediums are only people, and whatever decisions they might make about their work they are the ones who will have to live with the consequences when their conscience begins to prick.

As to mediums making money out of bereaved people, I have heard this levied at sensitives before. Does the minister get paid for taking a funeral service? Does the undertaker commit the remains of a loved one for no payment? Do doctors have a wage?

Are prayers answered?
It's not possible to give a clear-cut answer to that question, but I would say here that in many cases, yes they *are* answered but *not always in the way expected or as immediately as expected*. Prayer is a stream of *spontaneous*, living thought, born of desire. And someone, somewhere, will hear those thoughts. Just like a pebble dropped into a still pool of water, thoughts are born and radiate outwards.

Some requests, however, are so futile, so materialistic in their substance, that I doubt these would bring a response from any advanced Being in the Beyond. In the main, requests which will benefit soul-growth or some kind of good service towards others tend to bring the most fruitful and obviously visible results. But, of course, the Universal Laws stipulate that by the very act of prayer, the very act of opening the heart and seeking help from a Higher Source, the person praying is making him or herself available to the great influx of inspiration waiting to be poured into the minds of all those who seek its help. In this way, prayer can be seen as a personal exercise of one's own spirit, seeking its refreshment, guidance, or aid from those who are in attunement with it in Eternity.

By opening the heart, mind and spirit of one's own self to stimulating thoughts and energies, we can get in touch with the higher part of our nature, our higher mind, and in this way be healed and renewed to face our lives afresh.

How should we act towards others in order to advance spiritually?
I don't think I can give a precise answer to that, because we all

operate at different stages of spiritual development. But, for your consideration, I would suggest:

(a) Try to be patient with yourself and others;

(b) Try to really understand yourself, and others;

(c) Through self-examination, attain peacefulness within, and radiate it;

(d) As far as possible, adopt the principle of harmlessness in your lives;

(e) Be truly kind and genuinely loving towards all Creation;

(f) Exercise moderation in all things;

(g) Think positively, and act likewise;

(h) Exercise tolerance towards yourself and others;

(i) Take responsibility for your thoughts and actions;

(j) Recognize that all things are passing, nothing remains in a constant state — life is movement and change;

(k) Change what you can, and gracefully accept that which you can't change;

(l) Love each other, and serve each other with a willing heart.

Stephen, why do you continue with your mediumship?

Because there are souls in the next life desperate to dry the eyes of those who grieve for them on earth. I carry on because I have been called by the spirit to serve and educate, to stimulate thought and to proclaim, in my small way, that to love is better than to hate, and that peace should be written in every heart and mind. I believe that might is *not* right and that materialism is a mental disease which leads to greed and selfishness, poverty and the breakdown of human dignity. And I hope that, by using my voice to cry out a message of hope and reassurance, I can suggest an alternative road — the roadway that one man spoke of many years ago. And like him, I too point to the sign at the crossroads which says:

Love One Another.

Windrush

Dead leaves billowing in the air,
  Blowing, fluttering, not by Chance;
  Windrush green trees all a-gently swaying,
Bright leaves clapping out an Ageless dance.

Mankind breezing down through Time,
  Twistering forward through Earthlife's Game;
  Windrush children seeking and searching,
Learning vital lessons with unimportant names:

Growing minds
  Not one of them the same,

Trying to figure out
  Why they came . . .

18

'Oh Great White Spirit . . .'

[White Owl delivers an Invocation.]

Oh Great White Spirit,
Thou who art Omnipresent and Omnipotent,
the Power which marks even the smallest sparrow's fall:
I raise up my mind in simple humility, as would a little child,
and through the act of prayer
I would seek Thy Blessing upon this, Thy work.
From the deepest and most innermost Realms of Light,
I ask that Thy Messengers may come forward
to guide and inspire all these efforts
which are undertaken so that man may know more of Thee
and Thy wondrous Laws of Life.
It was Thee who fashioned the Universe
in all its beauty and vastness;
and it was Thee
who brought into Being, the Mind of Man;
and linked him forever unto Thy Great Creative
Consciousness.
And for these Unending Gifts of Life,
we are eternally grateful.
And it is the Prayer of these,
Thy Peace-Loving Servants in the Spirit,
that this vital task of spreading
Knowledge of Thy Eternal Truths may continue;

and thereby reach every Soul
in need of Food for their Spirit.
This we ask of Thee.
And for all Thy Blessings,
hidden and seen,
we send Thee our grateful thanks.

19

Touching Souls

The train windows closed in on me and the passing countryside blurred into an unrecognizable streak. My head swam and buzzed and I felt uncontrollably sick. In a daze, I rose unsteadily from my seat and staggered along the aisles into the cloakroom — where I was violently ill. I felt I wanted to die. How I got back to my seat, I'll never know. There were flashing lights in my vision and I was mentally whirling into delirium. I didn't know what time it was; I didn't know where the train was — all I knew was that I needed urgent medical attention.

I dimly recall pulling a passing Guard's coat and begging for help. For six long, agonizing hours I'd suffered these pains, and my endurance was now spent. The next thing I remember I was being carried off the train onto a freezing-cold platform and strapped into an invalid's chair and wheeled embarrassingly into a Buffet Bar on the station.

I was hundreds of miles from home and over 50 miles from my destination. The last thing I needed was the piercing stares of nearby travellers, who all stopped sipping their teas and gawped at me, sniffing and sobbing in my wheelchair. What an humiliating experience! I just kept thinking, 'Why couldn't they put me in a private office?' as I wiped my eyes. I was so ill, so terribly unwell.

After 20 minutes of public scrutiny, and a series of loud and embarrassing questions by two ambulancemen, I was whisked into their vehicle and sped across the city to hospital. Too weak to stand, they carried me into a curtained-off room, put me in a loose gown and left me on a bed. I was ice-cold. The sickness and nausea were so bad, a Sister injected me in the thigh to ease the pain, and then left me alone. But I kept calling out for a nurse. 'In a minute,' she shouted from afar. But she was too late. I was violently ill, all over the scant bedding, the screens and floor. She came rushing across, skidding on the tiles, and muttering, 'God help him too. Poor thing.'

Too unwell to travel, they hospitalized me for the night, next to a suicide attempt on the left and a drugs overdose case on my right.

As soon as dawn came, I'd had enough. I signed myself out, and by seven o'clock that evening I'd travelled the extra 50 miles and took my public meeting — weakly, but nevertheless I'd kept my appointment with the Other Side. I wouldn't let them down.

Unfortunately, the following morning I had a sudden, gushing nose-bleed. There was blood everywhere and I had to be rushed to yet another hospital to have the wound cauterized! 'My God,' I remember saying, 'this hasn't been my week at all!'

For years I'd been travelling the highways and byways; and a great deal of my time was spent either on a train or in a trance! Countryside flew past, there were so many destinations: large cities, smaller towns, villages and hamlets — each one offering a wanderer like me a warm welcome.

Those close to me know I don't travel well. Train journeys can be boring, tedious and seem such a waste of precious time. They're often long with complicated connections, and on boiling-hot summer days, they're almost unbearable. But travelling isn't the only problem I've encountered. Sometimes I've had to endure intense public humiliation, too, because of my beliefs, like at the séance in Huddersfield held for a Paranormal Research Group, where two hostile sceptics were present among the other 40 that night. It was a table-tilting experiment, and we had to wait an agonizing 45 minutes for the spirit-power to lift and dance the table for us. Then our two aggressive guests accused everyone of pushing it and manipulating the phenomena. What an humiliating experience, to have to sit through a tirade of accusations like that. I replied: 'If we were pushing, don't you think we'd have moved it ages ago?' They eventually retracted their claims, but what was more unbelievable was that the people around the table were their friends!

In all my years of public appearances, I think I've only been heckled once. The heckler sat, legs apart, his lips folded in a tight, thin line and his beady eyes stabbing at me in the face from 30 yards away. People forget mediums are sensitive and I'd spotted him the moment I took the stage.

I'd only just started my address — I wasn't even into the communications when he suddenly shouted out: 'Rubbish!' from the stalls. He was so rude, so repeatedly aggressive, that the entire audience turned and rallied on him, ordering him to 'Shut up!' He really made quite a fool of himself. And when I continued very calmly and without the slighest trace of retaliation, the whole crowd burst into spontaneous applause. I suspect it'll be a long time before he tries to disrupt another meeting like that.

I sat down afterwards and thought to myself, 'Why on Earth do you do it, Stephen? The gruelling tours, the sniggering from the sceptics — why?' And then I remembered . . .

I'd been relaxing quietly in my armchair, when in an instant I'd left my body and was standing upon a plateau at the top of a high mountain in the Spirit Spheres. The air was crisp and clear, the spirit-heavens lit with a brilliant blue sky. On the horizon was a speck of distant colour. It was a human form, gliding towards me at incredible speed.

I stood steadfast and fixed my gaze upon the man coming to meet me. As he drew near, I felt a great peace enfold me. And there he stood tall; my 'friend' of long ago, White Owl.

I searched his face. How could he look so young and yet emanate a feeling of being so ancient? With an outstretched hand he touched my breast, and instantly my skin parted, revealing my beating heart. His soundless voice said: 'Open your heart.' I knew he meant: be compassionate. 'There are thousands who need your help.'

Then, all at once, I found myself floating up huge sandstone steps, heat rising from them under the brilliant sun. Together we glided upwards to the top of what looked like an Aztec temple. Then I became aware of lying flat-out on a sacrificial altar, my face toward the burning sun. My companion stood over me. With a ceremonial knife raised high above my form, in an instant, he plunged the blade deep into my breast. And as the blackness engulfed me, I heard the word 'sacrifice'.

The scene shifted again and I stood upon a platform before thousands of people, all awaiting my efforts to bring a message of peace and hope. There were seas of expectant faces, and others — so many queuing outside to get in. 'Why am I here?' I wondered. The answer was granted — it was a shadow of things to come. It was the future.

'Serve whenever you can, wherever you can,' sailed through my mind. His meaning was clear: a life dedicated to the service of others involves great personal sacrifices. And then my Guide's clear tones broke into my consciousness: 'Give of yourself and do not count the cost.' In that moment, I could see him standing close to me as I viewed the waiting crowds. And he told me I'd be given what was needed to complete the task. 'Trust and I will guide,' he said.

Then, as swiftly as a thought, a swirling grey mist enveloped the pictures. The ground fell away from underneath my feet and I was dropping down through space and time. And I rudely awoke in my chair to the sights of Mother Earth once more . . .

In my heart, a great realization was pounding. I'd been born to accomplish something — to point out a way perhaps? Yet I'd often fallen short of these great ideals. But now this should change. All those years ago when this Vision of Another World was granted to me, I knew I was setting my future path. In my mind, the road ahead was being framed and born. I knew it would be a way strewn with hardships, tears, laughter and indescribable joy. But nevertheless, with characteristic determination, I was going to walk it.

I had promised my 'friend'. We were an inseparable pair; a two worlds team . . .

It took quite a time before I realized that I'd joined the ranks of the 'recognized', so to speak. In fact, it was only when a young Midlands man said: 'Thank you for your advice. It's not often famous mediums take time to give that,' that it dawned on me. 'But I'm not famous,' I replied with a raised brow. Then when I thought about it, people from all walks of life had travelled from all parts of the world to attend conferences I was teaching at, and to seek some help. They'd come from America, South Africa, Holland, Germany and other European countries. And I remembered being stopped in the streets and spoken to by complete strangers. They'd smile and ask how I was. 'Fine,' I'd say. And when they'd gone I wondered who on earth they were! After one television appearance I was out shopping, unshaven and with my woolly hat pulled firmly down on my head to combat the cold; I must have looked a sight. As I passed a checkout I overheard three sales girls saying: 'He's a medium. I saw him on the telly last night.' So I dived behind a fixture and straightened my hat! I can't imagine why! No amount of straightening could improve it!

Having joined the 'known', I must admit I did find coping with recognition rather stressful. I am a very private individual, almost living the life of a recluse, and the public pressures just didn't sit well with me at first. It took a long time to learn to accept them gracefully. And something which helped that process were the touching letters that started arriving from all over the kingdom. And I was immensely moved when reading them. Such as the one from an 83-year-old widow from Stoke who wrote: 'I was very impressed and greatly helped by your meeting last night. You told us we should count our blessings, and that's what I've been doing all day. It's 33 years since my husband died and left me alone. You have no idea how important your work is to the many thousands like me. So may God bless you and all your efforts. And may the years ahead be very happy. My constant prayer is that you will be richly blessed.'

There was the touching letter from a family in Surrey. The daughter enclosed a gift of a tie, saying, 'My thanks to you for the happiness you radiated not only to me but to everyone who needs your help.' Her father wrote: 'I expect this is one of many letters you receive, but I don't think any are written with more sincerity. May the Divine Spirit guide you in your wonderful work.' And a Cleveland couple penned: 'You are prayed for each evening, that you may be kept well and go forward to greater heights, giving out compassion to so many who need you.' And they enclosed a donation for a Handicapped Children's Society and the NSPCC, which I was supporting.

Personal gifts were regularly sent to me; people were so very kind, especially the poorest of the poor, who exhibited the most thoughtfulness of them all. Gifts would often come with beautiful notes saying how much a small contact from a loved-one through me had changed the whole course of their lives and given them new hope to struggle on.

After many public meetings, people would flock towards the stage or wait in corridors just to get my autograph or have their pictures taken with me; something I've never fully understood, or condoned. Finally, organizers and stewards had to be placed at strategic points backstage, just to keep some privacy there for me to rest during appearances; and these 'bodyguards' had quite a hard time preventing some fervent admirers the access they demanded. Once, there was so much bother removing an insistent crowd from outside my locked dressing-room that I even considered escaping through a high window to go to my hotel in peace.

Some folks have gone so far as to want their children 'blessed'. 'Just hold him,' they'd say, and people pressed around me simply to touch me. I guess they thought it would help them in some way. One woman even confessed she'd often called upon my name when under stress and she'd been helped many times in this way.

'Please,' I'd remind them, 'I'm just an ordinary person, you know; please don't make me into something I'm not.' But I guess some people just don't want to listen, for at other times they've wanted locks of my hair — believing they might cure them of any ills — and I've also been asked to bless jewellery and even rosary beads. 'Say a prayer over them, and I know they'll carry some of your power to help me through my life,' said a gentle lady. I am never amazed any more.

Other requests were most welcome, such as the invitation to open and speak at a peace rally in Durham City, held to commemorate the remembrance of the 80,000 people killed in Hiroshima and Nagasaki in the Second World War. Prayers were said that this travesty caused through misuse of nuclear power would hopefully never happen again. Then people floated lighted candles down the river in memory of those lost.

Being in the public eye also meant that I got to meet fascinating people I never would have known otherwise; none were more intriguing than the holy man, Guru Sagar Swami. He floated up the garden path in his long, orange silk shift, his head shaved and his bright eyes shining with happiness. The neighbours must have had a real treat when he came to call with his attendant. They were both such a mystical sight.

For over two hours we discussed the vital issues of life and its meaning, each gaining knowledge from the other and challenging one another's viewpoints in true healthy fashion. And at the end of our meeting he turned and said: 'I give you an open invitation to my Temple, day or night. And I bless you with the name of Lotus-Mouth — he who speaks wisdom.' Well, for once in my life I was speechless! And Swami and his faithful attendant floated away again down the garden path!

Another most welcome visitor I met was not of this world. One afternoon I had a lovely surprise while listening to my music. I caught sight of something through the corner of my eye. When I turned, there before me stood world-acclaimed film actress, Judy Garland. I could barely believe my eyes. Here she was, petite and wearing a black skirt and jacket, red button earrings, and her hair was cropped short on the sides and swept up on the top of her head. She was a radiant picture of health, full of smiles and obviously pleased to have been seen. But suddenly her face darkened and she spoke. She told me she was worried about one of her daughters, Liza Minnelli. Judy was concerned that 'Liza might take the same path I went along myself'. And a second later, before I could question Judy Garland, she vanished.

Why did she appear to me in the first place? I was always fond of her films, but I didn't know her daughter, Liza, so what on earth could be the point of her contact with me? I had no way of checking her statement. Once again, the spirit-people had been quietly at work, not only to amaze me with her presence in my living-room but also to quite clearly make a point.

It was only two years or so later that Liza Minnelli's personal struggles at the Betty Ford clinic in California came to light and became public knowledge in Britain, fulfilling Judy's prediction and proving that people Over There have access to knowledge *out of our present awareness*. It was a powerful way of getting their message across. Despite which, it was smashing to see Judy Garland at such close quarters anyway.

I've had to learn to mix with the rich and famous in all walks of life, but that certainly doesn't mean that I belong to their income bracket! Some people think mediums are wealthy, yet nothing could be further from the truth. Hundreds of us drag ourselves out through rain and snow to serve, and we barely cover our travelling expenses. In my own case, I usually lost out. At my meetings, profits were donated to people in need or other registered charities, struggling desperately to try and survive in today's expensive world.

I can clearly remember the occasion when Lord Northampton — known by some in the House as the Mystic Marquis because of his interest in the paranormal — opened a seminar at a five-star hotel where I was to teach over 100 students. We dined opposite each other; me with barely a penny to my name, and he'd just sold a family masterpiece for eight million pounds! What a staggering thought. But my spirit-teachers have often told me, 'What counts are the treasures of the heart, not earthly wealth.' And I do agree with them.

As a medium, I've been invited to appear all over the globe, but too many commitments prevented me from accepting these kind offers. 'One day, I'll come,' I kept telling disappointed questioners. Even world-famous psychic artist, Coral Polge, received a polite refusal when she asked me to join her in South America. I gently declined, saying: 'Maybe you can bring me back some nuts from Brazil, Coral!' And we smiled good-heartedly about it, as friends do.

Coral Polge is the world's foremost psychic artist, and it's been my great delight to work with her, producing evidential messages for seekers. Coral, who is highly acclaimed for her drawings of spirit-communicators, has the portraits projected up onto a huge screen, and I give the evidence to place the links with audience members. One of her portraits was of an elderly farmer, and it had to be sent 1,500 miles to Poland by Mrs C. Wojciechowska to have it verified with the evidence as perfectly correct. It was her husband's grandfather.

We first appeared together before a sell-out audience of 650 people, and this was the happy start of many successful demonstrations as a team. Coral is a joy to work with; she's a lovely lady and has much credibility and integrity. One of the most memorable links we gave was when she drew a beautiful six-year-old girl with bobbed, blonde hair. I gave her name as Mary and a relevant surname, and then connected her with her brother in the crowd.

'She was one of eight children,' I said.

'No,' he replied. 'There were seven.' Then after a pause he corrected: 'Wait! There are seven left — she's the eighth!' The audience gasped. And then, after sending her love to her mother, the little girl gave the clinching evidence about dying in water. And her brother told the hundreds: 'She drowned in the bath.' What a happy man he was, after that contact.

Appearances on radio and television have also brought a good response from the public. Many are comforted or their thinking has been stimulated into new areas of thought. One amusing incident with the television people always sticks in my mind. It was at a large demonstration and the cameras had been set up all around the City Hall, including one on the stage, at the side, to view the expressions of recipients as their messages came through. I sat for a moment at a table while being introduced to the audience. With my eyes closed, I began to send out a request to the Other Side for their help, and quite suddenly I heard a crystal-clear voice whispering, 'Keep to the centre of the stage.'

'Good God,' I thought, 'the psychic power's fantastic tonight. That voice was as clear as a bell.' But when I opened my eyes — it was the cameraman giving me his instructions!

Sometimes, when appearing at theatres, radio stations also invited me to speak. One was Radio Bedfordshire, where I talked on the early-morning 'Breakfast in Beds' programme about my mediumship and what would happen at the sell-out demonstration that evening. One listener felt she *had* to ring the station and she expressed her gratitude for the comments I made. She said she was terminally ill, and that my words had brought her a sense of peace and comfort. And I felt so proud of my spirit-friends, for without them, none of my wonderful experiences would have occurred.

Meeting followed meeting. Audiences flocked to city halls and theatres, leisure complexes and centres. Many were turned away for lack of room as others gathered in their hundreds to hear the Message of Hope delivered by a World of Light. I've always instructed organizers to pack in as many investigators as possible, refusing no one the opportunity to hear the Message of the Spirit; and I've even had my own seat taken from underneath me for someone in the hall!

Some demonstrations aroused so much public interest that tickets completely sold out well in advance of the meeting. At one 1,000-seat venue in Neath Gwyn Hall, Wales, tickets sold out faster than for the world-renowned singing group The Three Degrees, who appeared there the following day.

Over a thousand gathered at a venue is a difficult number to handle sometimes. There are people *everywhere*; banked up all around me, to either side, and sometimes even behind me. Stalls and galleries blur under the powerful lights, and it's not easy to see where hands are raising to claim connections. So many faces, so many needs, thousands of hopes and expectations. I pray I can at least be given the strength and inspiration to meet some of them successfully.

At one particularly large theatre meeting, when I finished my clairvoyance, the crowd burst into unending enthusiastic applause; I sat down amid the noise. But they just kept on clapping wildly and I had to stand and take another bow. Then as the wall of sound raised around me, I gazed out at the smiling hundreds and immediately felt the presence of my unseen friend near to me. Mentally I thanked him, for his promises of long ago had all been kept. Here we were, standing together, touching souls and moving minds, while a happy, grateful audience washed us with waves of thunderous applause. And as the mighty sound echoed round the theatre, a kaleidoscope of emotional images clouded my thoughts: the tragic illness and early death of my mother; that thrilling moment when I took my first public meeting; then I saw hundreds of thank-you letters, and felt once more the desolation and utter loneliness of my wilderness years when I didn't know my pathway; TV camera crews and journalists appeared, clutching their note-pads; followed by the rich and famous, standing beside the destitute and poor. And through all of this, hundreds of clapping hands brought me back to the cheering crowd. And there, standing silently at the side of the stage, I saw a spirit-woman surrounded by glimmering golden light and dressed in shining white robes; and my heart leapt within me as I beheld the smiling face of my mother. And in her hands she carried one deep red rose . . .

Then White Owl's voice reverberated in my silent mind

again: 'Together we serve,' he said.

As a team we'd travelled countless thousands of miles. I'd met thousands of people; and despite the hardships and sacrifices involved, I wouldn't change it all for anything.

Someone once worked out that, so far, over 30,000 communicators have returned through my mediumship to get even a small word of hope to those who love them and miss them. And millions more through public meetings and television and radio appearances — however briefly — have heard the wonderful news that, whatever else happens to them in their daily lives, *they cannot die*.

And it has been my immense privilege, in some small way, to have helped that Great Truth to reach them.

20

The Beginning

The pattern is set and the work keeps flooding in. The telephone rings and promoters from London, Liverpool and Newcastle show great interest in bringing the Message of the Spirit through my mediumship to a much wider public day by day.

Glancing forward I can see television programme researchers getting in touch, nationwide media networks requesting interviews and hundreds of organizations wanting me to appear for them in their city halls and theatres to demonstrate that what the prophets of old taught is still true today: man is immortal and the Kingdom of Heaven is very close at hand — within us.

This morning's mail sits awaiting me. It'll take about two hours to answer it, I guess. Requests, thanks, expressions of deep gratitude for having shed a little light into dark lives — all these will need a reply.

I see there's one letter from the General Secretary of the PDSA, saying: 'I know that our Patron, Her Royal Highness Princess Alexandra would like me to thank you on her behalf for all the goodwill and support you have given to the PDSA.' But the pleasure was all mine.

The door still knocks, and when I open it I'm greeted by the same grief-stricken cry for help. The features and circumstances are different, but the plea is always the same: 'Please Mr O'Brien, I've lost someone who meant the world to me. My whole life is in pieces and I don't think I can go on. Please, can you help me?'

'Come on in and we'll have some tea and we'll see what we can do.'

But how can I possibly accommodate all these demands upon my time and strength? The answer is simple. I'll do what I can in the time God has given me. With His help I know I'll manage to achieve what I was born to do.

Thinking back, I've come a long way since those spirit-hands hammered on our front door in the early hours when I was just 10 years old. Only now, in retrospect, can I truly see the weaving of the pattern; how each thread has slipped into its rightful place, how each colour of the design has added depth and growth to the whole. There's been heartache, sorrow, grief and tears. There was a stirring search for love. But there has also been indescribable joy, laughter, happiness and, above all else, service. The great work of service to others has brought lasting friendships and a sense of purpose into my life.

And what White Owl told me all those years ago when we first became a team has come to pass:

> If together we can lift only one who lies fallen by the wayside, if we can touch only *one* soul and stir it into thinking, then our work will not be in vain. We can give solace to the lonely, knowledge to the ignorant and comfort to the bereaved through the great truth that sets man free.
>
> When spirit truths touch the hearts of men and women everywhere with the knowledge that might is not right and that materialism and selfishness are not the only ways, then the Great Spirit's children will slowly realign their thinking and bring out from within them the love that is there, and give it freely to all those in need.
>
> When this happens and peace reigns in your world, we in the spirit-realms shall sing for joy.

In a quiet moment, I asked him why he undertook this great mission, and he said he did it:

> Out of love for my brothers and sisters still encased in the flesh. I have walked your way. I know its sorrows and its trials well. When I was at my lowest ebb, when all seemed dark around me

in my life, from somewhere, someone came and held out a torch for me to find my way again. I have never forgotten those who gave up their time to help a humble 'uneducated' man towards inner happiness through the food of the spirit they gave me so freely. When I knew the opportunity was open for me to do likewise for others, I grasped it in both hands and approached the grey earth again.

Did I not say when we first united under the banner of co-operation that the way would not be easy? It never is for those who travel the path of service. But life is about growth. Learning, discovering, a journey through time and space, overflowing with human experiences that help the soul to find itself and wake up to its infinite possibilities.

Together we have helped many towards the light of knowledge. I promised we would. And what a great joy it is to know we have played our parts.

But I could not have done it without you. You have been my voice, my eyes and ears, my hands. In the time you have left to exist on earth, I sincerely pray our partnership will continue, my friend.

There is still much work to do, and few to do it. But on behalf of all the spirits linked together in our band of helpers here with me, we give you our undying thanks, and tell you — without any doubt — that we love you.

I went back to my hills and valleys of Wales just recently, thinking about this book and the events that led me to where I am today.

The old house where I was born no longer exists. It's just a distant dream now, and in its place stands a smart estate. My father lives in one of the houses there. Dad and I are now great friends. Those old disagreements are dead and gone and we're both older and, thank God, much wiser. We're becoming good pals at last. Someone once said that time is a great healer. And I think they're right.

'How are you getting on?' Dad asked.

'Fine thanks. How about you?'

'Oh, mustn't grumble.'

'No point,' I said. 'Tomorrow's the first day of the rest of our lives.' Then we walked to the front door, and I glanced over my shoulder and saw the top of the landing where my mother appeared to me in a blaze of light, three months after her death. And I wondered if she was with us both as we talked.

We parted company at the top of our steps. 'Take care of yourself, Stephen. You live so far away now, but don't forget, if there's ever anything I can do to help you, I will. You're my son.'

'Thanks Dad. And make sure you keep well.'

'Aye, I'll do my best.' And for the first time in my life, I leaned across and kissed my father on the cheek. 'Goodbye then, Dad. I'll come and see you again soon.'

'Goodbye, son.'

For old time's sake, I went strolling around my boyhood haunts — the school where my mother met me in bad weather, the park where I played as a lad — they're all still there. Standing in the parkland, I recalled my youth. And as the sun beat down upon me, the memories flooded in, and I remembered the woman whose love had started it all. The loss of my mother and her spirit-return changed the course of my life. Her voice calling to me from beyond death, her form appearing at the top of our staircase, the gentle kiss she gave — the many proofs of her survival and continuing care. All these thoughts filled my mind.

And as I stood there in the sunlight I knew beyond doubt that one day, when my life here is over, she will meet me at the gateway and we'll be together again.

Just then, I felt her welcome presence drawing close to me. And as faint as a whisper, I heard her voice say: 'What have you learned, Stephen?'

Without hesitation I replied: 'Many lessons. But for me, just one stands out in my mind. Only one single thought — just one code of conduct means more than anything else now.'

'And what's that, son?' she asked.

And breathing in the scented summer air, I replied: 'Without love we are nothing.'

'Stephen,' my mother whispered, 'the adventure is just beginning . . .'

And
When we stand
On the Shores of Eternity
And look back
Upon our Experiences
In Earthlife,
We will notice
How all the things we did
Happened
In just the right places,
At just the right times:

And
We shall say to Ourselves:

It is Good.